A BARTHOLOMEW MAP & GUIDE

WALK ROYAL DEESIDE & NORTH EAST SCOTLAND

INCLUDING ANGUS

40 WALKS SELECTED & DESCRIBED BY RICHARD HALLEWELL
ILLUSTRATIONS BY REBECCA JOHNSTONE

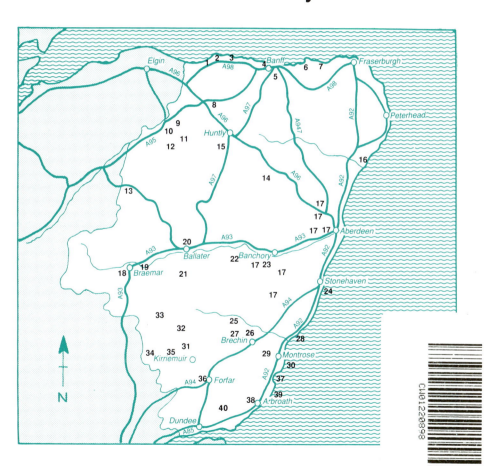

JOHN BARTHOLOMEW & SON LTD
EDINBURGH

British Library Cataloguing in Publication Data

Hallewell, Richard
        Walk Royal Deeside & North East Scotland
        (including Angus)
        1. Scotland. Grampian region. Visitors'
        guides
        I. Title
        914.12'104858

    ISBN 0-7028-0898-9

Published and Printed in Scotland
by John Bartholomew & Son Ltd.
Duncan Street, Edinburgh EH9 1TA

First Edition 1989
Copyright © John Bartholomew & Son Ltd, 1989

ISBN 0-7028-0898-9

The physical landscape of Britain is changing all the time
e.g. as new tracks are made, hedges grubbed up and fields
amalgamated. While every care has been taken in the
preparation of this guide, John Bartholomew & Son Ltd
will not be responsible for any loss, damage or
inconvenience caused by inaccuracies

About this book

This is a book of walks, all of which can be completed within one day. They pass through every type of scenery to be found in the area – hill, coastal and woodland – and vary in difficulty from gentle strolls to strenuous hill climbs. Each route is graded according to its level of difficulty, and wherever specialist hill-walking equipment is required this is specified. There is a description of each route, including information on the character and condition of the paths and a brief description of the major points of interest along the way. Some of the more interesting views are reproduced in annotated sketches. In addition there is a sketch map of the route to aid navigation. Car parks, where available, are indicated on the route maps; where parking is not mentioned it may be assumed that it presents no difficulties. The availability of public conveniences and public transport on particular routes is listed on the contents page, and at the head of each route. The suitability or otherwise of the route for dogs is also indicated on the contents page. The location of each route within the area is shown on the area map inside the cover of the book, and a brief description of how to reach the walk from the nearest town is provided at the start of each walk. In addition, National Grid References are provided on the maps. The use of a detailed map, in addition to this book, is advised on all A grade walks.

The following introduction provides a brief summary of the history and natural history of the North East, and lists people of consequence who have been associated with the area. Hopefully, an appreciation of these links with the past will add to the interest of the walks.

Before setting out, all walkers are asked to read through the section of Advice to Walkers at the end of this introduction. In the long term it never pays to become lax in taking safety precautions.

This is by no means an exhaustive list of the walks in this area, but it provides a core of varied, accepted routes. I hope you will find it an interesting selection.

Key

●●● Route	Marshland	**1 foot = 0.3m**
═══ Metalled Road	Moorland	**1 mile = 1.6km**
┼┼┼┼┼ Railway	♠♠ Coniferous Woodland	
ⓟ Parking	♠♠ Broad-leaved Woodland	
Contour: shaded area is above height indicated	*i* Information Centre	

The Area

(figures in italics refer to individual walks)

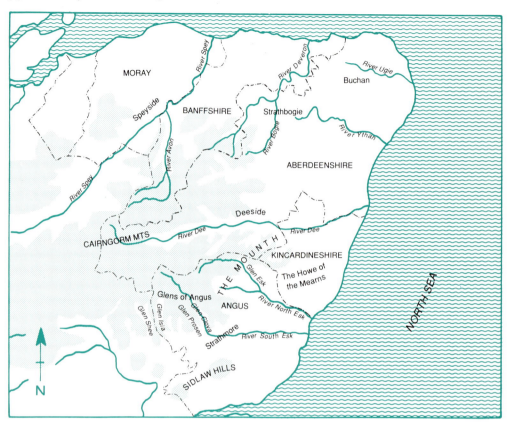

The area covered by this guide is large and diverse and, although it contains some of the finest walking in Scotland, the quality and nature of the landscape varies greatly. Some brief introduction to the North East, its geography, economy and history, is required if the visitor is to know where best to walk for the desired scenery or historical connections.

A glance at the map inside the cover of this guide shows the boundaries of the area covered, the positions of the main towns and the routes of the major roads. This should help to find individual walks, but some further description is needed of the great variety of countryside so crudely summarised by this map.

In political terms, the area is comprised of the old counties of Angus, Kincardineshire, Aberdeenshire (including the distinctive areas of Buchan and Deeside), Banffshire, and a small part of Moray. Since, for reasons which are partly practical and partly reactionary, I refer to these counties throughout the text (in preference to the bulky and drab 'regions' of Tayside and Grampian), I have included a map (above) illustrating their boundaries, along with some of the area's more important geographical features.

Starting from the south, **Angus** covers 855sq miles. It is bounded to the south by the Firth of Tay and to the east by the North Sea, and marches with the counties of Perthshire, Aberdeenshire and

Kincardineshire. The highest point in the county is the summit of Glas Maol (3502ft/1068m), where Perth, Aberdeen and Angus meet.

Geologically, Angus is divided in two by the Highland Line, a pronounced fault line running approximately along a south-west/north-east axis, from Helensburgh on the Clyde to Stonehaven in Kincardineshire. In Angus it runs along a line to the north-west of Kirriemuir and Edzell. The fault divides the area into a hilly, even mountainous, interior, largely comprised of metamorphic and igneous rocks, and a low, fertile, sandstone plain, broken by the low ridge of the Sidlaw Hills.

The plain is the more prosperous area, but the best walking – and it is some of the best walking in the country – is undoubtedly in the hills and glens above the Highland Line. Access to the hills is provided by the famous Glens of Angus: long, narrow, winding valleys, scraped out of the rock by glacial action during the ice-age, when the ice gathered in corries between the spurs of the Grampians and carved wide, deep, U-shaped valleys, which now dwarf the resident rivers. The view from Cairn Broadlands *(33)* down Glen Clova provides a perfect view of a typical glaciated valley, with its attendant hanging valleys and alluvial plain. It is not unique, however, and all the 'Highland' walks included in the book pass through similar landscapes.

The Angus glens cut through the hills in a south-easterly direction, crossing the Highland Line at a right angle; their rivers then flowing on towards the sea through the low farmland of Strathmore.

The rivers and the glens are, from north to south: the North Esk (Glen Esk) *(25)*, West Water (Glen Lethnot), South Esk (Glen Clova) *(31,32,33)*, Prosen Water (Glen Prosen) *(31)* and the Isla (Glen Isla) *(34)*. Most of these rivers experience a jolt as they cross the boundary fault, and along the Highland Line there are many fine waterfalls. The best in Angus are probably those in the hills behind the town of Edzell, where the River North Esk thunders through the Rocks of Solitude *(26)*.

The walks between the parallel glens, and

over the Mounth into Deeside, are too long – with the exception of the Minister's Path from Prosen to Clova *(31)* – to be included in this book, but they are too famous to be ignored, so the map below is included to show the routes of these longer walks: 1) Tolmount/Jock's Road; 2) Kilbo; 3) Glen Prosen to Glen Isla; 4) Capel Mounth; 5) Minister's Path; 6) Clova to Glen Esk; 7) Ballater to Glen Esk by Mount Keen; 8) Firmounth; 9) Fungle; 10) Clash of Wirren. **None of these routes should be attempted by inexperienced walkers: they are long, high and rough.**

After rushing from the hills, the rivers slow down as they meander through the rich farmland of the broad valley of Strathmore. The Isla cuts south and joins the Tay north of Perth; the others flow east, eventually reaching the North Sea – the North Esk (including West Water) at St Cyrus *(28)* and the South Esk (including the Prosen) in the broad, muddy bowl of Montrose Basin *(29)*: a curious, round estuary; dry at low tide and a fine place for bird-watching.

Strathmore is an area of great, placid, beauty; with many fine houses, broad, tree-lined fields, and prosperous towns and villages; perhaps seen at its best from the roads over the Sidlaws, just as the mist is rising from the fields on a late, autumn afternoon. This is a fine, civilized place, although there is little walking.

The main towns of Angus are all in the lowland area: Montrose and Arbroath on the coast, and Brechin, Forfar and Kirriemuir in Strathmore, while the City of Dundee sits on the Firth of Tay, beyond the Sidlaw Hills to the south.

Dundee's position is unrivalled: facing south across the broad estuary of the Tay (the 'Silvery Tay' of William McGonagall: one of Scotland's many bad poets, but the only one who is famous for it) spanned by the road and rail bridges, and with the green fields of Fife beyond. Sadly, the city itself remains rather unattractive, and has suffered the misfortune of being commercially becalmed in the very worst phase of urban development. However, it has a certain vitality, and a rich industrial past, founded, as the saying goes, on 'Jam, Jute and Journalism', plus other minor industries, including whaling. Although Aberdeen and Peterhead also had whaling fleets, Dundee's was the largest in the area; largely because the jute spinners required the whale oil to mix with the fibre and make it easier to work. Dundee's association with the whale fishery ended with the virtual disappearance of the Bowhead Whale in the early 20th century.

Fishing, if not whaling, is still carried out from Arbroath *(38,39)*, up the coast, and the harbour area retains the invigorating bustle of a working port. Montrose, to the north, is more concerned with oil than fishing, and the main part of the town, squeezed between Montrose Basin and the sea, turns its back on the ocean. It is an elegant settlement with many interesting corners and a certain timeless charm; perhaps the legacy of its long, largely tranquil history. Montrose's past is one of trade, rather than warfare.

Forfar *(36)*, Brechin and Kirriemuir are pleasant, country market towns. Brechin is elevated to the status of a city by its cathedral (largely 13th-century, but rebuilt in the 20th century), by the side of which is an even older religious building: a curious round tower, 87ft/27m high, built in the 10th or 11th century. The only other example of such a structure in Scotland is at Abernethy, in Perthshire, although there are many in Ireland. Their purpose would seem to have been, at least partly, defensive.

Kirriemuir is famous as the birthplace of JM Barrie; the author of *'The Admirable Crichton'* and *'Peter Pan'*, whose father was a linen weaver in the town. Barrie recreated Kirriemuir in an idealised form as 'Thrums'; a half imaginary town which featured in many of his early, romantic, stories. Barrie's birthplace, in Brechin Road, is now owned by the National Trust for Scotland.

In earliest recorded history, Angus was part of the southern kingdom of the Picts (separated from the north by the Mounth: the eastern arm of the Grampian Mountains). Nothing much remains of the Picts except a few short references in the histories of other nations, and a few carved stones – the only certain cultural relics of their society – but they must once have been a considerable nation.

They were called the 'Picti' or the 'Caledonii' (from which 'Caledonia', and place names such as 'Schiehallion' *(Fairy Mountain of the Caledonians)* in Perthshire) by the Romans, who defeated them at Mons Graupius, somewhere in eastern Scotland, in AD 84, and who subsequently considered them dangerous enough to require the building of the Hadrian's and Antonine Walls. In later years the Picts struck a decisive blow against the expansionist Northumbrians, who had been making inroads into Angus from the south. At the Battle of Nechtansmere (on Dunnichen Hill, near Forfar), in AD 685, King Brude and his Picts drew King Egfrith's army into an ambush; killing the king and destroying his army.

Subsequently, under the military pressure of the Viking raids, and the cultural pressure of the Gaelic church, they merged with the Gaelic-speaking Scots of Dalriada, under Kenneth MacAlpin, in AD 843. Within a short space of time their language and culture had completely vanished. Some political links with the past remained, however; most obviously in the use of the Scottish east coast as the main power centre, and the retention of Pictish area names. These had originated as the domains of the 'mormaers' – sub-kings beneath the rulers of Pictland – and were subsequently transformed into Earldoms. Examples include Moray, Buchan, Mar and Angus; all area names which are still in use, to varying extents, today.

The engraved symbol stones of the Picts – the later examples with relief religious images, and the earlier with incised diagrammatic animals and curious, distinctive symbols which have now lost all meaning – are common throughout the whole area; some lying in churchyards (which they may often predate) *(11,15)*, others on the grassy verges of roads (such as the Maiden's Stone, at Bennachie *(14)*, and the stones at Aberlemno, near Brechin), while others have now been collected into museums. The best collections are in the Museum of Antiquites, in Edinburgh; Meigle Museum, near Alyth; and St Vigeans Museum *(38)*, in Arbroath.

In the centuries following Pictland's eclipse, Angus's agricultural wealth ensured that it remained an important theatre in Scottish affairs. In 1296 King John of Scotland (John Balliol) was forced into an uprising against his feudal overlord, King Edward I of England. The uprising ended in shambolic defeat at Dunbar, and Balliol fled north, followed by the English. He received the swingeing conditions of surrender at Brechin, and signed away his kingdom in Montrose.

This act of national humiliation was rectified, 24 years later, by one of affirmation, when the Declaration of Arbroath was signed at Arbroath Abbey (now ruined) in 1320. The Declaration took the form of a letter to Pope John XXII, and contains some stirring, plangent passages – *For so long as there shall but one hundred of us remain alive, we will never consent to subject ourselves to the dominion of the English. For it is not glory, it is not riches, neither is it honour, but it is liberty alone that we fight and contend for, which no honest man will lose but with his life.* By this time, of course, Bruce had led his successful war of liberation and was an independent monarch.

Three hundred years later there was civil war throughout the British Isles, between the Stewart kings and the forces of Protestantism: in Scotland the Covenanters. Two of the Royalist cause's finest generals came from Angus; both from the house of Graham.

In the 1640s James Graham, Marquis of Montrose, led a small army of Highlanders to a series of stunning victories throughout northern Scotland, before being defeated at Philiphaugh in 1645, and eventually captured and executed in 1650. During his life he was considered one of the finest soldiers in Europe, and Wishart's Latin rendering of his campaigns – later translated into English and French – was widely read. Montrose's great appeal has always been the blend which he displayed of martial efficiency, iron nerve and high-minded loyalty; and also that capacity to inspire loyalty in others which is common to all great generals. One of the Angus families who most resolutely followed Montrose were the Ogilvies (the Earls of Airlie); a connection for which they paid dearly when, in 1639, the Earl of Argyll, a staunch Covenanter, destroyed Airlie Castle.

In the 1680s John Graham of Claverhouse, later Viscount Dundee, was a supporter of Charles II and James VII. He died whilst trying to emulate Montrose's feats; leading a Highland army against the Covenanters at Killiecrankie in 1688. The battle was won, but Dundee was killed in the moment of victory, thus ending the campaign.

To the north of Angus is the county of **Kincardineshire**; the smallest county in the area (379 sq miles). Kincardineshire is on the North Sea coast, bordered to the north and north-west (partly along the line of the River Dee) by Aberdeenshire, and to the south and south-west by Angus (along the River North Esk). The county includes the ridge of the Mounth; the most easterly spur of the Grampian Mountains, which finally peter out within a few miles of the coast, leaving a narrow strip of low land which the major lines of communication have always been forced to follow. There are hill trails to the west, and one road (the old military road by Cairn o'Mount (B974), which climbs to a height of 1475ft/455m)), but most armies – including Edward I (twice: 1296 and 1303); Montrose (1645: he burnt the town of Stonehaven) and the Jacobite armies (1715 and 1745) – and other travellers, were forced to follow the coastal route. Near the narrowest point (and at one end of the Highland Line) are the port of

Stonehaven and, more important historically, the cliff-top fortress of Dunnottar *(24)*.

Stonehaven was the county town of Kincardineshire, and is now the headquarters of Kincardine and Deeside District Council. The town was largely the work of two powerful local families: the Barclays of Ury and the Keiths. The head of the senior line of the Keiths bore the title Earl Marischal, and was the keeper of Dunnottar.

Dunnottar was, for many years, the principal fortress of the North East, and was fought over fiercely during Scotland's various wars. It was taken from an occupying English force by William Wallace in 1297; in 1645, the Earl Marischal watched from his battlements as Montrose – an ally in the forces of the Covenant six years previously – burnt every stick of his estates; in 1651 General Overton laid a successful seige against the castle for Cromwell; and in 1715 the castle was denuded of cannon for the Jacobite army.

Overton's seige had a specific purpose which was thwarted by one of those romantic acts of loyalty (usually unrewarded) which are so common in the history of the relationship between the Scots and the Stewart monarchy. Dunnottar was the strongbox which held the Scots Regalia – the Scottish crown jewels – and Charles II's private papers. The seige began in September 1651, and by the time the governor of the castle, Sir George Ogilvy of Barras, left Dunnottar, with the full honours of war, both papers and regalia had been spirited away; the latter having been lowered to the beach below the castle and smuggled away in a basket of seaweed. They lay beneath the pulpit of nearby Kinneff Church until the Restoration.

To the south of Stonehaven and the south-east of the Grampians is the Howe of the Mearns; an area of intensive farming, characterised by its heavy, red, sandstone soil, and immortalised in the books of Lewis Grassic Gibbon, who was born and lived his early life in the low hills behind Inverbervie.

Inverbervie is one of a line of small towns and fishing villages on the south Kincardineshire coast: St Cyrus, Johnshaven, Gourdon, Inverbervie and Catterline. This last, and smallest, was, for some years, the home of the artist Joan Eardley (1921-63) who, in order to capture the mood of the the stormy, violent seas of the North Sea coast, would paint on the shore with the corners of her canvas held down by rocks.

Behind this coastal strip is the long, low, Hill of Garvock, from which there are fine views across the Mearns to the mountains beyond.

North of Stonehaven, the sandstone gives way to metamorphic rocks, and the landscape becomes more hilly. In the north-east of the county, at the north end of the Cairn o'Mount road, is the large, open town of Banchory *(23)*, at the eastern end of Deeside.

To the north of Kincardineshire is **Aberdeenshire**; the largest and most diverse of the area's counties. The south-western corner is taken up by the mountainous country around Deeside, which marches with Angus to the south, Perthshire to the south-west, Invernessshire to the west, and Banffshire to the north. The River Dee takes its headwaters from the Cairngorms, a range which includes many of the highest peaks in Scotland (including Cairn Toul, Braeriach and Ben Macdhui, which mark the county boundary). The dramatic pass of the Lairig Ghru follows the headwaters of the River Dee northwards, through the highest peaks of the Cairngorms to Aviemore on Speyside.

The hills to the south of the Dee are little less impressive, and include Lochnagar and Glas Maol. It is a most dramatic region, and the only exits, except on foot, are eastwards, down the Dee towards Aberdeen, or southwards, on the A93 through Glenshee from Braemar *(18,19)* to Strathmore.

Historically, Deeside's remoteness left it one of the most Gaelic areas of the North East, despite the difficulties of direct communication with the Gaelic-speaking heartland to the west. As a result, the most powerful families in the valley – Farquharsons and Gordons – were as much Highland clans as they were Lowland families.

The main Farquharson houses were at

Inverey, near the end of the narrow road which leads up to the falls at the Linn of Dee, and Invercauld, to the north of the river near Braemar, where the present chief still lives. Braemar Castle is another Farquharson house; this one a 17th-century tower house –a cruder form of the elegant Renaissance towers further east – with an angled, star-shaped barmkin and later, decorative, crenellated towers. The castle is open to the public, and one is instantly, and unexpectedly, struck by the cosiness of the place. An interesting feature are the carved names of 18th-century Hanoverian soldiers who were billeted in the building in the wake of the Jacobite uprisings.

East of Braemar, and due north of the summit of Lochnagar, is the tiny village of Crathie. To the south of the river, opposite the village, is the royal holiday home of Balmoral, surrounded by the light-brown and bottle-green of the Scots pine, which are so distinctive a feature of Deeside.

Balmoral was bought by Prince Albert in 1852, and the castle rebuilt in a mock Scots Baronial style to his requirements. The grounds of the castle are generally open to the public.

East of Balmoral is the old spa town of Ballater *(20)*, and beyond that Dinnet, Aboyne, Kincardine O'Neil and Banchory. To the south of Deeside, leading into the hills, there are three main glens: Glen Muick, to the west, including Loch Muick *(21)* – part of the royal estates, and overshadowed by the bulk of Lochnagar to the north-west; Glen Tanar *(22)*, with its fine pine woods; and Glen Feugh, behind Banchory.

To the east of Banchory there is a low land of mixed farming, forestry and housing: the satellite towns of Aberdeen. There is little walking in this area, but it does contain the finest examples of one of Scotland's great cultural legacies: the Scots Baronial tower houses of the late 16th and early 17th centuries. Essentially, these are Fraser, Crathes, Fyvie, Craigievar and Midmar; all but the last now owned by the National Trust for Scotland, but historically the property of branches of the Fraser, Burnett, Seton, Forbes and Gordon families respectively.

These masterly compositions were largely the work of a family of master masons called 'Bel', of whom, sadly, little is known save their work; though that is enough to show them the equals of Scotland's other great architectural dynasty, the Adams, who worked in the 18th century.

The smallest of the castles is the best; indeed, it is one of the finest buildings in Scotland. Craigievar was built in 1626 for William Forbes – a highly succesful Baltic trader known as 'Willy the Merchant' – and, of the castles listed, it alone has remained free of later additions, and stands today largely as its builders intended.

The basic form of the castles was that of a traditional Scottish defensive keep, but the comparative prosperity and political stablility of the time allowed patrons to compromise on simply defensive needs. Craigievar exemplifies this compromise – between harsh necessity and Renaissance fantasy – perfectly.

The castle sits in a wooded valley in the low hills between Deeside and Strathdon. Pale-pink harled, the L-shaped tower rises straight-sided and self contained for the first four storeys, then erupts in the final three into a mass of turrets, gables, balustrades and cupolas.

The main settlement in the North East is the city of Aberdeen – euphemistically called the 'Silver City by the Golden Sands' because of the predominant use of the pale, cold, local granite in its major buildings and the city's fine, sandy beach. Aberdeen has reached prominence in recent years through the off-shore oil industry, but it has been the hub of the North East for centuries, and boasts many fine old buildings: including King's College Chapel, begun in 1500 but with later rebuilding work; the 16th-century Provost Skene's House; the 19th-century Art Gallery, and many other fine, early 19th-century terraces and houses; plus the massive and elaborate Marischal College building, completed in 1906, in which the local granite has been carved into an improbable mass of tiny pinnacles. Marischal College was founded in 1593, by George Keith, 5th Earl Marischal, and is one of the two constituent colleges of Aberdeen University; the other being King's College (1494). Marischal was set up specifically as a Protestant alternative to the older college.

The religious intolerance inherent in such decisions reached its height, in Scotland, during the wars of the Covenant, and Aberdeen received more than its share of troubles during the period. The city had the misfortune to be taken twice by Montrose; once, during the Bishop's War, when he was fighting for the Covenant forces, and a second time, in 1644, when he fought for the king. After the second battle, his victorious Irish and Highland troops sacked the town for three days; killing any Covenanters they found, and many civilians besides.

Aberdeen straddles two major rivers which reach the North Sea within $2^1/_2$ miles of each other: the Dee and the Don. Deeside is well known, but Strathdon is less so, for, though very beautiful, it lacks the grandeur of its neighbour.

The river originates in the host of moorland hills to the north-east of the Cairngorms, and winds through its shallow glen into the farmland of the Howe of Alford, and on, past the towns of Kemnay, Inverurie and Kintore, into the suburbs of Aberdeen.

North of Aberdeen, the golden sands by the cold North Sea continue: 15 miles in all from the mouth of the Dee to The Sands of Forvie *(16)*, north of the Ythan estuary. Behind the sands spreads a lumpy patchwork of farms and roads.

North of the Ythan, incorporating the north-eastern point of Aberdeenshire, and spreading as far west, historically, as the River Deveron, is the area of Buchan. The name no longer has any political significance, except as part of the Banff and Buchan District of Grampian Region, but the term is so widely used, and the area so individual, that it should be noted.

Like most of the North East, Buchan was, until comparatively recently, a rough, poor, bleak land. In the late 17th century, some attempts began to be made to extract more from the peaty soil and now the area is as heavily cultivated as any in Scotland. Inland, Buchan is comprised of a flat, windblown plain, largely treeless and with only the occasional hill – in particular the Hill of Mormond, south of Fraserburgh, with its NATO

early warning system and its huge white horse, 160ft/49m in length, made of white granite stones. Scattered across this landscape there are a multitude of farms, and a number of small, self-contained towns: Crimond, Strichen, New Pitsligo, Maud, Mintlaw and, on the River Ythan, Ellon.

On the east coast are the small villages of Cruden Bay (where Braham Stoker wrote 'Dracula'; in part inspired by his evening walks to the ruins of Slains Castle) and Boddam, to the south of the port of Peterhead. Through industry and foresight Peterhead has become a major port; the huge boom across the mouth of Peterhead Bay provides a sheltered outer harbour for vessels involved in the oil industry, while the inner harbour complex now comprises the largest white fish port in Europe. There is nothing to beat the atmosphere of a working port, and Peterhead works full time, with its dockside fishmarket, ice-factory, boat slips, ship-chandleries and the endless coming and going of fishing boats. The rest of the town is of limited attraction, but the harbour is pure pleasure.

Further north, around Buchan's terminal bulge (Rattray Head and Cairnbulg Point), is the port of Fraserburgh; close behind Peterhead and Aberdeen as a fishing port. Who does not envy the opportunity of the landowners of the past to build their own towns? – such as the planned villages at Laurencekirk (Lord Gardenstone), Ballater (Francis Farquharson), Cullen (the Earl of Seafield), and Dufftown (the Earl of Fife). These were all 18th-century creations, but Peterhead and Fraserburgh were started much earlier: Peterhead in 1593, by George Keith, 5th Earl Marischal, and Fraserburgh (previously Faithlie) by Alexander Fraser of Philorth in 1546, whose descendents presided over the growth of his town. In 1595 a university was started but, sadly, this failed in 1605 for political reasons.

To the west, along the coast, is the old fishing village of Pennan *(7)*, in a rare break in the cliffs which line the coast. This is one of a line of handsome coastal towns and fishing villages which stretches as far as Nairn. Many are on the sites of very old settlements, from where local subsistence fishing has been carried out for centuries, but the main thrust of expansion in the North East fisheries occurred in the 19th century, when the herring fishery took off in earnest. Old photographs show the harbours of Scottish fishing towns, from Eyemouth to Lerwick, packed with boats like herrings in a box. It was a boom time such as the north of Scotland had never seen, and only the bustle of Peterhead and Fraserburgh can come close to recreating the atmosphere of these small towns when, for example, the tiny village of Sandend (in Banffshire) could send 35 boats to the fishing.

The last corner of Aberdeenshire to be covered is Strathbogie: the land around the River Bogie – a tributory of the River Deveron. The area is one of mixed forestry, moorland and farmland, on rolling, rounded hills around narrow valleys.

The centre of Strathbogie is the handsome town of Huntly, in the angle between the Bogie and the Deveron. This is another planned town; this time built by the most powerful of all the families in the North East, the Gordons; and laid out in the 18th century in the grid-iron pattern typical of the day.

At the north end of the town are the ruins of Huntly Castle: for long the central point in the web of estates, intrigues and interlaced families which were the business of the Gordons throughout the north.

As has been said, the North East was a bleak and unprosperous area until comparatively recent times; self-contained and far from the centres of power to the south; as much involved in Highland affairs as Lowland. This poverty and seclusion allowed a very small number of families to dominate a huge area and, in the history of the North East, the names Gordon, Keith, Hay, Irvine, Ogilvie, Forbes, Farquharson and Fraser invariably appear in the thick of any action.

Before 1314 this list would have been dominated by the Comyn family, but their senior line stood between Robert the Bruce and the Scottish throne. Bruce killed his two main rivals in Dumfries in 1306, and then, having defeated the

Comyn Earl of Buchan at Inverurie in 1308, ravaged his huge estates. This prolonged burst of slaughter and destruction is remembered as the 'Herschip (harrying) of Buchan', and was essential if Bruce was to ensure that his back was clear when he headed south for further confrontation with the English.

Many of the families who were subsequently strong throughout the North East received much of their land in the area in the wake of the wholesale disinheritance of the Comyn family which followed Bruce's victory at Bannockburn. Beneficiaries from this redistribution included the Irvines and the Burnetts (the Forest of Drum), the Hays (Slains Castle), and the Keiths (large estates to the north of the Ythan).

A list of the roots of the more important families in the North East gives a good shorthand account of the foreign intrusions into the area during Scotland's blustery history. The Comyns, Hays and Frasers were all descended from aristocratic Anglo-Norman families who came to Scotland in the years following William the Conqueror's victory at Hastings in 1066, encouraged by a succesion of Scottish kings who used Norman families to bolster their power. The Farquharsons were descended from the Shaw clan, in the Gaelic west. Forbes and Ogilvie are Pictish place names, apparently adopted by local families, while Keith and Gordon are place names in the south of Scotland, adopted by families who subsequently moved north to lands granted for services to the crown or acquired through marriage.

The only invasion not reflected in this list is that of the Vikings, who made comparatively little lasting impact on the North East; preferring to colonise the lands of the far north and the Western Isles.

The role of the Gordons in the North East was similar to that of the Campbells in the south western Highlands: that is to say, they were used by successive monarchs as law enforcers over the troublesome smaller clans in the adjacent Highland areas. Both families used their powers to expand their wealth, lands and prestige, and, if anything, the Gordons' greater distance from authority left them a greater leeway and independence.

One of the many branches of this extensive family were the Gordons of Gight (a castle on the River Ythan, north-west of Haddo House). In 1785, the heiress of this turbulent family, Catherine Gordon, married 'Mad Jack' Byron – heir to an equally erratic blood-line – and produced George Gordon Byron, who, by good fortune in the death of his relatives, came into an English Baronetcy and estate, and went on to conquer the world with his poetry. It is fashionable to see Byron as a Scottish poet. He lived his early life in Aberdeen and visited Deeside when convalescing from scarlet fever (precociously falling in love with a neighbour at the age of eight), and he wrote some verses in praise of his childhood haunts, but it seems silly to claim for the cause of patriotism a man who clearly had no thought of it himself. Nonetheless, he stands as a typically eccentric and brilliant example of his maternal clan.

The county of **Banffshire** sits to the west of Aberdeenshire and covers 630 sq miles; mountainous in the south, where the border reaches the peak of Ben Macdhui in the Cairngorms, and flat in the north, where farmland runs down to the Moray Firth. The county's main rivers are the Deveron, the Avon and the Spey. The Deveron flows north from the hills south-west of Strathbogie into Banff Bay, and forms part of the eastern boundary with Aberdeenshire, while the Avon takes its headwaters from the highest of the cairngorms and then flows northwards to join the Spey (Scotland's second longest river after the Tay), which forms part of the county boundary with **Moray**. The part of Moray east of the Spey is included in the scope of this guide.

The line of coastal villages which starts in Buchan, to the east, continues along the Banffshire coast: Crovie, Gardenstown, Macduff, Banff, Whitehills and Buckie still house fishing fleets. These towns and villages are amongst the most splendid in Scotland; the rows of fishermen's cottages often painted in bright colours. This was originally done to waterproof the buildings, and has now become a most picturesque tradition. The eastern villages of Crovie and Gardenstown *(6)* are the most dramatic: the former squeezed into a narrow space at the foot of the high cliffs which line the coast; the latter clustered tightly on the steep slope behind Gamrie Bay; the road zig-zagging through the houses down to the harbour.

The fishing boom of the 19th century, which saw the growth of many of those settlements, was based upon the abundant herring – the 'silver darlings' –and made possible by the railways. The herring, which swims in vast shoals in the cold nothern seas, is a mysterious fish; following a pattern of migration which means it can be caught in the north in the early summer, and in the south by the autumn. The larger fishing boats from the Scottish ports would migrate with the fish through the summer, selling their catches at the nearest port, before returning northwards in the autumn. This was only possible in the most seaworthy vessels, and it took some years to develop the perfect design.

Initially, the fishermen of the North East sailed in 'Scaffies' – single masted open luggers – and hugged the coastline, but a series of storms in the 1840's convinced the industry of these vessels' fundamental shortcomings, and a larger boat, the 'Fifie', was adopted. Then, in 1879, the first 'Zulu' was built in Banff. The Zulus – so called after the Zulu War – were the finest sailing fishing vessels ever built in Scotland: up to 70ft/21m in length, with two huge lug sails set on immense, unstayed masts made of Norway pine. The design was fast, strong and seaworthy, and old photographs confirm the Zulu's reputation for being one of the most elegant sailing vessels ever designed. The age of progress allows for little sentimentality, however; within 40 years these splendid craft were superseded by steam.

Fishing aside, the most important traditional industry in Banffshire is malt whisky production. There are distilleries throughout the area, but the quarter where they lie densest is Speyside, and at the centre of the Speyside malt industry are the towns of Aberlour *(10)*, Craigellachie *(9)* and Dufftown *(9,11)*. It warms the heart simply to read the place-names on the map: Glen Fiddich, Glen Livet, Mortlach, Ben Rinnes *(12)*. No one is quite certain why Scotch Whisky should defy all attempts at imitation, but it does. Some influence of water, grain or peat has proved impossible to reproduce anywhere else, to the lasting financial benefit of the area.

Apart from the fishing villages, and the handsome old county town of Banff *(4,5)*, the main centres are at Keith *(8)*, Dufftown and, in the hilly south of the county, Tomintoul *(13)*: 1200ft/360m above sea-level, and at one end of the infamous Cock Bridge to Tomintoul road: the spiralling A939 linking Speyside with Strathdon.

The Gordon family were prominent in Banff and Moray, and the strange story of the succession of Findlater *(3)* provides a perfect example of the often contrived means by which they attempted to augment their estates.

The 16th-century laird of Findlater, Alexander Ogilvie, had a wife who was a Gordon, and a son – James, his only direct descendant – by an earlier marriage. John Gordon, a son of the Earl of Huntly, decided to trick the Ogilvies out of their estate. He told Alexander that James was planning to drive him (Ogilvie) mad, by locking him up and depriving him of sleep, and contrived, with the connivance of Ogilvie's wife, to convince the laird that he should leave the estate to him (Gordon) instead. On Ogilvie's death Gordon took control of Findlater Castle, and strengthened his grip on the inheritance by marrying Ogilvie's widow; only to have her locked up shortly afterwards.

On this occasion all ended 'happily', with Mary Queen of Scots returning the estates to the Ogilvie heir, and Gordon being executed for his part in a subsequent insurrection.

Place Names

A list of some of the common elements in the place names of the area is given below. Some names – generally those of larger features, such as rivers – are so old as to be impossible to translate. These names usually date from the pre-Celtic era, and the languages spoken then have either been absorbed into modern languages, or completely forgotten. Equally forgotten is the language of the Picts.

The Picts were the earliest inhabitants of eastern Scotland for whom recognisable place names exist. The extent of their habitation would seem to be defined by place names with the suffix 'pit' (thought to mean a 'piece of land'). This conclusion appears to be verified by the almost identical range of occurence of the Pictish symbol stones, which are the only objects which can be reliably traced back to Pictish culture. Since 'pit' names occur throughout the area covered by this book, one can reasonably assume that the Picts lived throughout most, probably all, of the area covered; an assumption which tallies with the existing historical evidence, which would suggest that the area included covers some, or all, of three

of Pictland's seven provinces: namely 'Angus and the Mearns', 'Marr and Buchan' and 'Moray and Ross' – all names which have survived to the present day.

In AD 840 Kenneth MacAlpin became king of both Pictland and Dalriada: the homeland of the Scots on the west coast. How he achieved this ascendancy is not clear, but within a short period the culture and language of the Scots had completely obliterated that of the Picts.

The Scots came originally from Ireland, and spoke Gaelic. This entire area contains Gaelic place names, and it is clear that the language was universal throughout northern Scotland for a period of three or four centuries.

In the 9th century, the Viking attacks began on northern Scotland but although there are records of attacks and battles in the North-East, there are no Scandinavian place names, and the area appears not to have been colonised.

The first intrusions of the Germanic languages came with the Northumbrian advance in the 7th century, but following the Picts' victory at the

Battle of Nechtansmere, in Angus, and the subsequent withdrawal of the invaders, it was some centuries before Germanic speakers began to penetrate north of the Tay. When they did so, they spoke not English but Scots: a dialect so extreme that it was on the verge of becoming a separate language when the advent of mass communications (the printing press) heralded the modern era of creeping uniformity. Nonetheless, the majority of place names in the low-lying, agricultural sections of this area (these were the areas where the incoming language spread most rapidly) include elements which are recognisably Scots.

The area is now almost entirely English speaking (though still in a patois which outsiders may find it hard to penetrate), with a few Gaelic remnants in the far north and west. Gaelic was still widespread until comparatively recent times, and the degree of corruption of the original Gaelic in an individual place name is evidence of the time that has passed since it first ceased to have a specific meaning, and became instead a symbol in a foreign language: Gleann an t-Slugain, north of Braemar, was obviously a Gaelic-speaking area more recently than Balnamoon in Buchan. As a rule of thumb; the more difficult a place name is to pronounce, the nearer it is to the original Gaelic.

The following list includes elements from all the languages listed above.

Common Elements of Place Names

Aber – *Confluence*
Ach – *Field*
Allt – *Stream*
Aonach – *Steep slope*
Bal – *Town, settlement*
Beag, beg – *small*
Ben – *Mountain*
Blair – *Plain*
Brae – *Slope*
Breac, breck – *Speckled*
Bruach – *Slope*
Burn – *Stream*
Cairn – *Hill, heap of stones*
Ceann – *Head, end*
Coire – *Corrie*
Craig, creag – *Rock, cliff*
Den – *Narrow glen*
Drochaid – *Bridge*
Drum – *Ridge*
Dubh – *Black*
Dun – *Fort, steep hill*
Elrig – *Deer trap*
Fauld – *sheep-fold*
Firth – *Arm of the sea*
Garbh – *Rough*
Gouk – *Cuckoo, fool*
Haugh – *Flat land by river*

Inch – *Flat land by river or small island*
Inver – *River-mouth, confluence*
Iolaire – *Eagle*
Howe – *Hollow*
Kil – *Church*
Kin – *Head, end*
Kirk – *Church*
Knock – *Hill*
Law – *Hill*
Links – *Sandy grassland near shore*
Linn – *Waterfall or pool at base of fall*
Loan – *Lane, path or small common*
Lochan – *Small loch*
Mains – *Main farm*
Meall – *Hill*
Meickle – *Great*
Monadh – *Moor*
Mór – *Large*
Nether – *Lower, next*
Ness – *Headland*
Neuk – *Corner, crevice, angle*
Rig – *Ridge or long, narrow hill*
Ruadh, roy – *Red*
Sron – *Nose, promontory*
Strath – *Valley plain*
Tom – *Hill*
Tulloch – *Hillock*

Natural History

The variety of landscape in the North East is very great; ranging from the damp, cold, exposed peaks of the Cairngorms (where the climate is sub-arctic and the plant life alpine) to the cliffs, dunes and mud flats of the estuaries and coasts; and including coniferous and broad-leaved woodland (both natural and commercial) and grazing and arable farmland.

This range of habitats provides cover for a large number of bird and animal species; some of which – due to the extreme conditions on the high tops and the comparatively low density of population throughout much of the area – are unlikely to be seen in the rest of the country.

A number of the routes in this guide run through nature reserves *(16,18,21,28,29)*, and there are others throughout the area, but the wildlife is generally abundant, and sightings of interesting species can be expected at any time, along any of these walks.

The area can usefully be divided into a number of environments which recur along the routes – **Commercial Forestry, Woodland, Hills and Moorland, Farmland, Freshwater, Seashore** – and the bird, animal and plant life typical of each can then be listed. This has been done below. Routes which particularly feature each environment are listed beside the headings. Naturally, it is impossible to be entirely accurate with such a brief study, and great good fortune is required to see some of the rarer and shyer species, but this should give a rough indication of the type of thing which may be seen along the way.

Commerical Forestry *(14,17,19,22,23,33,40)*
These plantations are of comparatively little interest to naturalists. They provide cover for **rabbit, fox** and **roe deer**, but the trees are generally packed close together, thus keeping sunlight from the forest floor and inhibiting the undergrowth necessary to sustain the smaller animals and insects at the bottom of the food chain.

The trees planted are quite varied. The list includes not only native **Scots pine**, but also **lodge-pole pine, Sitka** and **Norway spruce; Japanese, European** and **hybrid larch; Douglas fir** and others; developed from the basic species to produce trees which grow straight and fast.

The bird life of the plantations can include **blue, great** and **coal tits, bullfinch** and **chaffinch, crossbill, siskin, crested tit, jay, wood pigeon** and **long-eared owl**. However, sightings can be difficult because of the close packed branches.

Most forestry plantations include areas of broad-leaved woodland. In these areas the species present are likely to include those listed in the **Woodland** section.

Woodland *(5,8,9,10,11,18,20,22,26)*
The range of this category is very wide, and it includes a number of different types of natural and semi-natural woodland: pine forest, birchwood, oakwood, etc.

The **Scots pine** is the only conifer indigenous to the British Isles. It arrived in northern Scotland some 8000 years ago, following the retreat of the glaciers, and at one time forests containing little else covered much of the Highlands, up to height of some 3000ft /900m above sea level, while the glens and low ground were covered in broad-leaved forests. Nowadays, the pine forest exists in only a few, small, protected pockets; particularly in Speyside, Glen Affric and Deeside.

The disappearance of the original forests was partly due to climatic changes, which seem to have reduced the pine's ability to regenerate. It is still not uncommon to see stands of old trees with no younger ones coming through beneath, although there are now encouraging signs of regrowth in areas such as Glen Tanar *(22)*, and Bennachie *(14)*.

The Scots pine is a hardy tree, but it is sensitive to differences in climate and soil, and reflects these differences in the shape which it adopts. In a well-protected glen *(22)*, or when grown in commercial plantations (as it is in much of Deeside), it will grow straight and tall while, in an exposed position, it can become gnarled and twisted; lower and broader. On poor soil, or at heights approaching its limit (around 1500ft/ 750m), it can last many years while hardly growing at all, and if its position is both high and exposed (as with the scattered trees on Ben Rinnes *(12)*) it can crawl through the heather, almost like a shrub.

The tree is seen at its best in Glen Tanar: tall and straight, its bark becoming a very pale brown, almost pink, near the top of the tree, and its needles a deep bottle-green.

A typical pine forest consists almost entirely of the one type of tree, interspersed with occasional birch, rowan and alder. Birch is particularly common in the damper areas. Except in commercial plantations **heather, mosses** and **shrubs** generally grow beneath the trees.

The bird life is similar to that in the **Commerical Forestry**, listed above, plus **wood warbler** and **spotted flycatcher.**

Birchwoods are common throughout the western half of this area. There is no shortage of birch, and it is likely to be seen on any of the higher level walks, but there are two places in the area worthy of particular note. The first is Muir of Dinnet, north of Dinnet, in Deeside, where a large area of land around Loch Kinord has been set aside as a Nature Reserve, and where there is considerable regeneration of both birch and Scots pine. Further west, on the hills behind Braemar, another Nature Reserve has been established for the Morrone Birch Wood *(18)*: a high woodland of **birch, mosses** and **juniper**.

In low-lying areas the cover becomes more varied. Along these walks the densest tree cover tends to be found in narrow glens, where the land is useless for any other purpose *(8,9,10,11,26)*. A great range of trees is present, including **oak, beech, alder, ash, hawthorn, gean, rowan, willow, sycamore, holly, horse chestnut** and others. The finest trees passed along these routes are probably those around Duff House *(5)*. In addition, there is a fine oak wood on the southern face of Craigendarroch *(20)*.

Hills and Moorland

(12,14,15,18,21,25,27,31,32,33,34,35)
The area covered by this book climbs, on its

western edge, to the peaks of the Cairngorms – some of the highest hills in Scotland – but they are not covered by any of the walks because of the difficulty of approaching the range from the east. All the moorland walks included are therefore in the hills between Deeside and the Glens of Angus, with the exceptions of Bennachie *(14)*, Tap o'Noth *(15)* and Ben Rinnes *(12)* to the north.

Scotland's moors are one of its greatest glories: the heather giving a purple shade to the hillsides from July to September. The moors may appear empty, but they are of considerable interest to naturalists and are a central part of the economy of Highland areas – as sheep runs, grouse moors and deer forests – so be careful not to distrub the wildlife, and always check with estates, tourist information offices and local people before walking off the accepted moorland paths from August onwards, when grouse shooting and deer stalking are in progress.

The plant life which constitutes the moors varies greatly, depending on which direction the moor slopes, its height above sea level, and the underlying rock or soil. Flat areas of moorland are often 'floating' on a considerable depth of peat: a mass of black, sodden, half rotted vegetation. Peat moors tend to be very wet, and bogs and pools of dark water often develop. These moors largely exist on the higher plateaux of the hills *(12,32,34,35)*, and the plant life is broadly comprised of **ling heather, blaeberry, crowberry, cloudberry** and **mosses.**

Parts of the moors – particularly, in this area, on the hills of Angus – are burnt in the spring, to encourage new growth in the heather to feed both sheep and **red grouse**. The grouse moors in Angus are particularly fine, and the grouse can often be seen on the higher routes; springing up from the heather and flying off swiftly, giving a strange nasal call. Other birds to be seen on the moors include **skylark, wheatear, carrion crow, lapwing** and **curlew.**

Red deer are unlikely to be seen in the summer months, as they stay high in the hills when the weather is warm, but they return to the lower moors in the autumn. Around Loch Muick *(21)* the deer are fed by the wardens; as a result they are less shy than most and can usually be seen quite easily.

Fox and **stoat** are present on the hills, as they are throughout the area, and also the **mountain hare**, which can often be seen in quite large number. The mountain hare is slightly smaller than the comon variety, and, like the stoat, it turns white during the winter to assist camouflage.

Another creature which camouflages itself against the winter snows is the **ptarmigan** – the hardiest of the grouse family. This bird rarely ventures below 2500ft/750m, but may be seen on some of the higher walks, particularly in colder weather.

The birds of prey in this area include the **buzzard, peregrine, kestrel** and **hen harrier,** any of which might be seen on the hills; while the **golden eagle** may be spotted in the remoter glens.

One unmistableable bird is the **short-eared owl**; the only owl which is likely to be seen swooping over the moors in broad daylight.

Farmland *(3,7,22,30,35)*

A substantial part of this area is given over to farming. Starting from Strathmore in the south, a strip of low, fertile land runs up through the Howe of the Mearns, and on into Buchan; then west, along the coast of the Moray Firth. Inland, thin lines of farmland follow the floors of the valleys into the hills. The farmland in the area is divided between arable land in the more fertile areas, and livestock grazing elsewhere.

Having said this, not many of the routes included pass through farmland; simply because the more interesting walking is generally on the rougher ground.

Fields which are lined with hedgerows are usually home to **finches, sparrows, robin, linnet, wren, blackbird, thrushes** and others. Larger birds to be seen in the fields include **magpie, lapwing** and **curlew** (particularly in the higher fields) **pheasant** and **partridge**; plus **redwing** and **fieldfare** in the winter months. Watch for **swallow, swift** and **martins** during the summer.

There is a great variety of plant life along the hedgerows and the roadsides, including **knapweed,** **scabious, ragwort, cranesbill, ragged robin, cuckoo flower** and **red campion**, to name only a few.

Smaller mammals may occasionally be seen around the farms.

Freshwater *(9,10,11,21,22,26,29,33,36,40)*

This is a rather broad grouping, covering bogs, moorland burns, wooded dens, Highland lochs and broad rivers. A considerable amount of water falls on Scotland, and it all has to go somewhere, so most routes pass some water, running or still; only those in which it is a central element, however, are listed above.

On the moors there are reedy bogs, which seep into small burns, or perhaps into high lochans like Loch Brandy *(32)*. However high these lochs are, they always seem to attract **gulls** during the summer months.

The small hill burns flow through steep-sided, narrow glens, and mossy, ferny pools, into woodland dens *(10,11)*, surrounded by broad-leaved trees. Some larger rivers continue to flow through similar cover *(5,9,26)*.

There are few large inland lochs in the area, and the only one which is passed on these routes is Loch Muik *(21)*.

Duck are common at all stages of the rivers' development, with **mallard** and **teal** as high as the moor's edge, and **wigeon, pochard, goldeneye, red-breasted merganser, tufted duck** and **goosander** in the upper waters.

Also by the upper waters are **redshank, curlew, ring ouzel** and **lapwing**; while **dippers** and **grey** and **pied wagtails** are common by the wooded waters, and **coot, moorhen, dabchick** and **great-crested grebe** may be seen on still water.

The variety of freshwater fish in nothern Scotland is not great, but this deficiency is made up for by both the quantity and quality of those which are present. The most common is the **brown trout** – resident in most bodies of water – and the most imporant is the **Atlantic salmon**, which ascends the rivers during the summer to spawn in the headwaters at the end of the year. These fish can be seen jumping in rivers throughout the area. The

Spey is probably the most famous of the north's salmon rivers, but the Dee and the rivers of Angus are all productive.

Salmon is, of course, particularly noted as a game fish, but it is also netted commerically along the coasts, and salmon nets are a feature of a number of the coastal walks *(16,28,37)*.

There are few mammals which specifically live by the water, but one – the **otter** – is present in the area, although it is rare to spot one. Other swimmers include **water vole** and **mink.**

Seashore *(1,2,3,4,6,7,16,24,28,29,30,37,39)*
The seashore covered by the routes in this book can be divided into cliffs *(1,2,3,6,7,24,38)*, sand beaches *(1,2,3,4,7,16,28,37)*, rocky foreshores (along parts of the Moray Firth and south of Ferryden *(30)*), and the muddy Montrose Basin *(29)* which forms the estuary of the River South Esk.

Montrose Basin is of particular interest to birdwatchers. The mud supports large numbers of shellfish and small sea creatures, which in turn attract a great many birds: **mute** and **whooper swans; grey-lag** and **pink-footed geese; mallard, shelduck, wigeon, teal, tufted duck, shoveler, pintail, pochard, goldeneye, goosander** and **red-breasted merganser; oystercatcher, curlew sandpiper, dunlin, knot, redshank, sandpiper** and **curlew.** In addition, there are a great many **eider**; a species common along the length of the coast (as many of those listed above are), and present in particularly large numbers on the Ythan estuary *(16)*.

On the cliffs there are **puffin, guillemot, kittiwake** and **razorbill.** Also found by the coast are **cormorant, heron, common** and **Arctic terns**

(with breeding sites at St Cyrus *(28)* and Forvie *(16)*, plus a wide range of **gulls**.

The plant life of the shore includes **lichens** and **seaweeds**, and a variety of plants which are inured to the salty conditions, such as **sea-pink, sea-milkwort, scurvy grass, bird's-foot trefoil, sea-plantain, sea-sandwort, lyme grass** and **marram.** The last two species are vital along sandy coasts, where they help to stabilise the dunes.

General
Many of these species are shy and sensitive to intrusion, so it is important to disturb them as little as possible. The walker is in no danger from the wildlife of the area, although, as a general rule, it is wise to stay clear of any creature with young.

Of the domestic animals, **sheep-dogs** can be a nuisance, but are generally harmless; **bulls**, on the other hand, should never be approached, however lethargic they may appear.

There is one poisonous snake in the area – the **adder**. It is rare to see one – usually coiled in a patch of sunlight, somewhere quiet – and even rarer to be bitten. Adders are extremely shy and will always move if they sense someone approaching. Anyone who is bitten should consult a doctor. Bites are not lethal, but they give rise to an unpleasant, temporary illness.

The insect life of the North East is tame compared to that of the West Coast, but **midges** are always common when the weather is warm – particularly around areas of marshland or water – and can make life very uncomfortable. There are a number of creams and sprays to deter them, but they are extremely persistent.

Advice to Walkers

Always check the weather forecast before setting off on the longer walks and prepare yourself for the walk accordingly. Remember that an excess of sunshine – causing sunburn or dehydration – can be just as debilitating as snow or rain, and carry adequate cover for your body when on the hills.

Snow cover on the higher slopes often

remains well into the summer and should be avoided by inexperienced walkers as it often covers hidden pitfalls which are likely to cause injury. Also, when soft, snow is extremely gruelling to cross and can sap the energy very quickly. Walking on snow-covered hills should not be attempted without an ice-axe and crampons.

The other weather-associated danger on the hills is mist, which can appear very swiftly and cut visibility to a few yards. Such conditions should be anticipated, and a map and compass carried while on the higher hills.

Obviously these problems are unlikely to arise on the shorter, simpler routes, but it is always wise when out walking to anticipate the worst and to be ready for it. The extra equipment may never be needed, but it is worth taking anyway, just in case. Spare food, a first-aid kit, a whistle and a torch with a spare battery should be carried on all hill walks. In addition, details of your route and expected time of return should be left with someone, whom you should advise on your safe return.

There is one final danger for hill walkers which is entirely predictable. From August onwards there is grouse shooting and deer stalking on the moors. If you are undertaking one of the hill routes then check with the local estate or tourist office before doing so, thereby avoiding a nuisance for the sportsmen and possible danger to yourself.

Country Code

All walkers, when leaving public roads to pass through farmland, forestry or moorland, should respect the interests of those whose livelihood depends on the land. Carelessness can easily cause damage. You are therefore urged to follow the Country Code:

Guard against all risk of fire

Keep all dogs under proper control
(especially during the lambing season –
April/May)

Fasten all gates

Keep to the paths across farmland

Avoid damaging fences, hedges and walls

Leave no litter

Safeguard water supplies

Protect wildlife, wild plants and trees

Go carefully on country roads

Respect the life of the countryside

1 Buckie to Findochty

Length: 3 miles (5km) one way, from centre of Buckie
Height climbed: Negligible
Grade: B
Public conveniences: Findochty, Buckie
Public transport: Bus service along coast

A short coast walk between two fishing harbours.

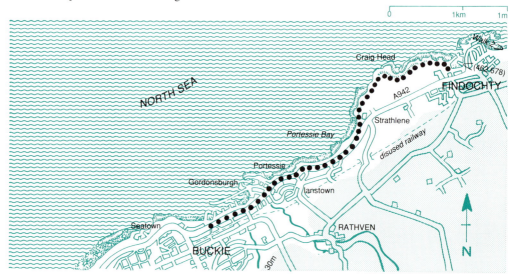

Buckie is a large fishing town on the coast of the Moray Firth; a small conurbation of villages – Buckpool, Seatown, Yardie, Gordonsburgh, Ianstown and Portessie – which amalgamated as they enlarged at the height of the Scottish herring boom in the 19th century. It is interesting to walk along the front at Buckie – it has a coast frontage of some three miles – and spot the architectural differences between the rows of small cottages, often end-on to the sea, which were the heart of the original villages, and the fishing buildings and the more prosperous housing of the 19th century which join them together.

The large harbour was built in 1880, and established Buckie as one of the most important fishing harbours in the north. Despite the subsequent retraction of the industry fishing remains important to the town today.

Walk east from the harbour along the

waterfront and, when the road cuts inland at Strathlene, cut down to the shore and continue along the coast; at first by a sandy beach, and then along the rocky coast towards Craig Head.

It is approximately a mile along the coast – past bays, inlets and caves – to the smaller village of Findochty. This is a most picturesque village, and the small, neat, cottages clustered around the harbour are – in the tradition of this corner of the country – painted a variety of colours.

There was some fishing from the village at least as early as the 16th century but it did not take off until 1716, when the local landowner brought men from Fraserburgh to fish from his harbour.

2 *Findochty to Cullen*

Length: 4 $\frac{1}{2}$ miles (7 km) one way
Height climbed: Negligible
Grade: B
Public conveniences: Findochty, Portknockie, Cullen
Public Trasnport: Bus service along coast

Coastal walk on beach, cliff-top and rough track. Fine villages, caves and scenery

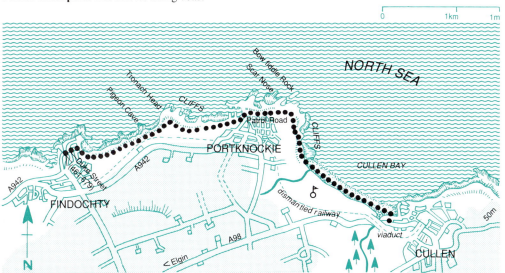

This is a fine, cliff-top walk, passing three of the small harbour villages, with their rows of painted cottages, which are one of the most pleasing architectural features of the area.

Starting from Findochty, walk eastwards from the harbour and leave the town by Duke Street. At the end of the street there is a sandy beach, with a view of the cliffs beyond. For those interested in caves, the excellent Pigeon Cave, high and airy with three large openings, and a fourth, smaller, hidden in the cliffs, burrows through a headland half a mile along the rocky foreshore.

Otherwise, cut up to the top of the low cliffs and follow the clear path through the gorse and bracken along the high cliff-top. A mile east of Findochty, as the path rounds Tronach Head, a view opens up to Portknockie; a grid-iron of fishing cottages on the nape of a headland, well above the little harbour. Leave Portknockie by

following Patrol Road along the northern edge of the town. Just beyond the houses there is a fine view from the cliff-top, down to the Bow Fiddle Rock: a massive stratified block, sunk in the water at 45°, with an arch of eroded rock clinging to its eastern face.

Continue along the cliff-top. After a short distance the town of Cullen comes to view at the far end of a long, sandy beach. Its old rail viaduct is prominent. The path curves around the headland and then leads back towards Portknockie. At this point a steep path, with steps, cuts down the face of the cliffs to the foreshore and then on to the beach. It is a further mile of easy walking to the edge of the pleasant town of Cullen.

3 Cullen to Portsoy

Length: 7 miles (11km) one way
Height climbed: Undulating
Grade: A
Public conveniences: Portsoy, Cullen
Public transport: Bus service along coast

Coastal walk on cliff-tops and beaches. Fine harbour towns and rugged scenery. Tracks rough.

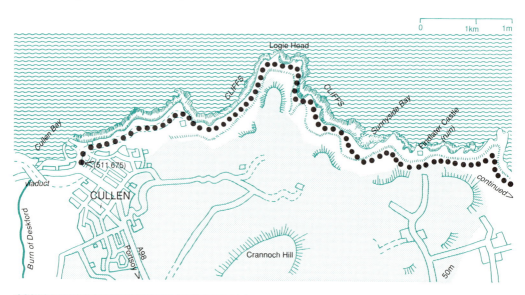

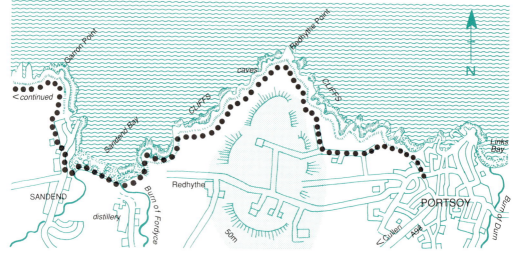

Walk 3

There is a string of small burghs and fishing villages running along the south side of the Moray Firth, from Nairn in the west to Fraserburgh in the east. Most reached the peak of their importance during the fishing boom in the 19th century – the result of an expanding population and the advent of the railways, providing a large market and the swift delivery of fresh produce – but many were in existence before that, and have histories which are interesting quite apart from their association with the fisheries.

There has been a village in the area of Cullen since the 12th century, but its exact position has been changed through the years. At first it stood at Invercullen – near the mouth of the Burn of Deskford – but it was subsequently moved inland, and by the 19th century it had been established for some time around Cullen House (one mile inland by the burn side). In the 1820s the Earl of Seafield demolished the old town, and had a new one built a short distance to the north-east, behind the coastal fishing community at Seatown, which had been in existence since the early 17th century. The two distinct halves of the town – the wide main street and open square of the new town, and the clustered cottages of Seatown – are now divided by the grand sweep of the disused rail viaduct.

Start walking from Cullen harbour: eastwards, below the low cliffs, along the coast. The path is quite clear; out of rocky Logie Head, and on to the sands of Sunnyside Bay. From the bay the path climbs up from the shore to the cliff-top. A short distance beyond are the ruins of Findlater Castle, the 15th-century seat of the Ogilvies of Findlater. The crumbling masonry is perched on the edge of a high, rocky outcrop from the cliff. It must have been an uncomfortable residence for, despite its obvious strengths, it was abandoned in the late 16th century and the family moved to the newly built Cullen House in 1600.

A mile beyond Findlater, along the cliffs, is the tiny, exquisite fishing village of Sandend, at the west end of a broad, sandy beach. A number of fish curers still work in the village but it is no longer the fishing centre which it once was.

The rows of small cottage are lined up behind the beach and the tiny harbour; each row end-on to the sea, with a narrow alley in between. This formation ensured the maximum protection from the elements.

Walk along the beach to the east; past Glenlassaugh Distillery, at the foot of the Burn of Fordyce, and the adjacent ruined windmill, and on, through low grassy hills and along the rising cliff-tops, to Redhythe Point.

The path is rough in some places throughout this walk, and disappears completely in others, but for most of the way there is no difficulty with the route. A short distance after rounding Redhythe Point it leaves the cliffs and cuts inland, along a rough track. When this track reaches a junction turn left, then follow the track ahead into Portsoy.

Like Cullen, Portsoy is a substantial town; sitting at the head of a shallow bay, near the mouth of the Burn of Durn. The town was of some importance from as early as 1550, when it was made a burgh, and has a fine old harbour, built in 1692 by Patrick Ogilvie, Lord Boyne.

Ogilvie's plan was to develop the port for the export of the local Portsoy marble, and a number of 18th-century buildings around the harbour attest to the early success of this venture. Portsoy marble was even exported to France for use in the Palace of Versailles.

The town expanded again in the 19th century, when it became a vigorous fishing port. A new harbour was built to cater for the increasing number of boats.

Fishing is no longer carried out from Portsoy, and the vein of marble is worked only in a small way, but it remains a fine town, full of the idiosyncratic charms of Scots vernacular architecture.

4 Banff to Whitehills

Length: 3 miles (5km) harbour to harbour
Height climbed: None
Grade: C
Public conveniences: Banff, Whitehills
Public transport: Numerous bus services to
Banff, plus a connection between the two towns

*A short coastal walk between two harbours.
Path good*

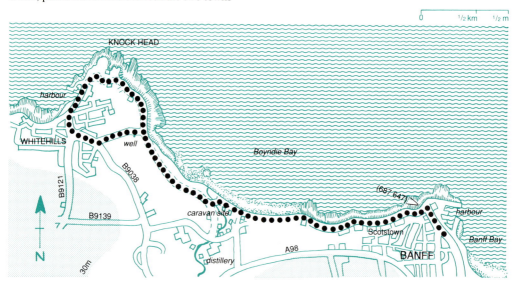

The town of Banff – the old county town, and now headquarters of Banff and Buchan District – is one of the finest on the northern coast, although it lacks the bustle of the ports – such as Macduff and Buckie – which are still actively involved in the fishing trade. Banff was a trading port from the 12th century but, along with the rest of the coast's harbours, underwent its greatest growth during the fishing boom; lasting, in Banff's case, from 1775 (when the first harbour was completed) until the end of the 19th century.

Start walking from the harbour, now largely used by pleasure craft, and head westwards, along the road by the waterfront, past the row of fishermen's cottages at Scotstown, and on to the beach at Boyndie Bay, which is backed by a caravan park. At the far end of the park cut left, over a footbridge across the Boyndie Burn, and continue behind the now rocky foreshore.

Ahead, a few of the houses of Whitehills are visible in the depression behind the mound on the end of Knock Head, which protects the harbour from the east. As the path starts to curve to the right, towards the point, it splits. The left hand track leads past a whitewashed beehive hut, containing a small spring, and on into the village; the longer, right hand path rounds the point and enters the village by the harbour.

Whitehills is unusual in that, despite its small size (the population is under a thousand), a fishing fleet still operates from its tiny harbour – though not the 100 boats which sailed from the village at the height of the herring fishing.

Return by the same route.

5 Duff House

Length: 6 miles (9.5km)
Height climbed: 250ft (70m)
Grade: B
Public conveniences: Banff
Public transport: Bus service along coast

A walk on good racks and metalled roadways through woodland and farmland about the River Deveron.

Banff is a handsome town by the mouth of the River Deveron. It was an important trading port from as early as the 12th century, and there was a castle on the site before that; while in the 18th century, the town became a fashionable resort. The harbour is now largely unused – the main fishing port on this stretch of coast is at Macduff, across Banff Bay – but there are still many splendid buildings in the town as reminders of the burgh's heydey. The most imposing of these is Duff House.

To start this route, follow the road to the golf course, from the east end of the town. After a short distance the road splits. Walk half left, across an area of parkland, to Duff House (the right hand track leads to the car park).

The house was begun in 1735 by William Adam for William Duff, the 1st Earl of Fife. It is a magnificent building, built in the Palladian style but with an unnaturally narrow frontage: this is because the planned symmetrical flanking pavilions were never built, due to arguments between patron and architect.

A woodland walk has been laid out in the Deveron Valley to the south of the house, through mixed trees of massive height and girth, to the elegant single-span Bridge of Alvah, built in 1772, over the broad, shallow ravine of the river. Cross this and follow the road through the farmland beyond to join the public road. Cut left, and then left again by a cottage, down a straight track through woodland and grazing land to the Duff Distillery near the east end of the seven arch Banff Bridge (1780).

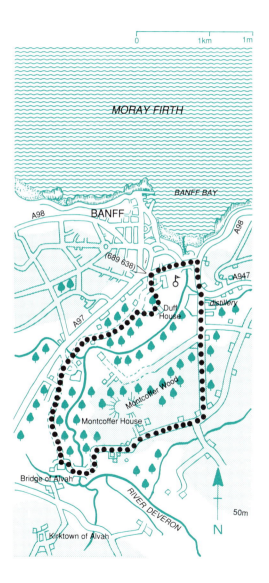

6 Gardenstown to Crovie

Length: 2¹/₂ miles (4km)
Height climbed: 450ft (140m)
Grade: C
Public conveniences: Gardenstown
Public transport: Bus service from Macduff

A short shoreline walk between two pleasant villages. Back by the public road.

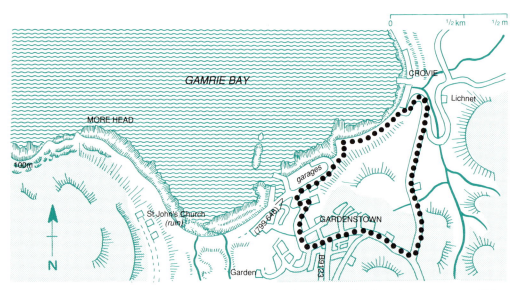

Gardenstown is an attractive old fishing harbour on the northern coast, looking on to the Moray Firth; 6 miles east of Macduff on the B9031. The town was founded by Alexander Garden of Troup in 1720. He chose one of the few places on the coast where the cliffs relent and allow access to the shore but, even here, the slopes are steep and the road zig-zags down through the houses which cling to the hillside above the harbour. To the west and east the cliffs rise steeply around the headlands on either side of Gamrie Bay. On a ledge on More Head, to the west of Gardenstown, are the remains of St. John's Church. Before it was abandoned, the church was decorated with the skulls of Vikings: a reminder of one of the less successful Norse raids in the North East.

Park in Gardenstown and start walking eastwards, through the garages at the end of the town. At the start of the coast path there is a sign warning of rock falls from the steep, grassy cliffs behind the beach. The way is clear and not difficult. Almost immediately there is a view of Crovie, less than a mile along the coast: a splendid row of fishermen's cottages, most of them built end-on to the sea, and many with wooden shutters to protect the windows. In common with many of the cottages along this coast those at Crovie are painted: pink, green, brown, slate-grey or blue.

Either return by the same route or follow the single-track road which climbs up the steep hill behind the cottages and continues through the farmland behind the coast. After a little under a mile this road reaches a junction. Cut right to return to Gardenstown.

7 Pennan to New Aberdour

Length: 3 ½ miles (5.5km) one way
Height climbed: 500ft (150m) undulating
Grade: B
Public conveniences: New Aberdour
Public Transport: Limited bus services to both towns from Frasburgh and Banff

A lineal path through farmland near coastal cliffs; from a delightful harbour to a fine beach. Paths rough.

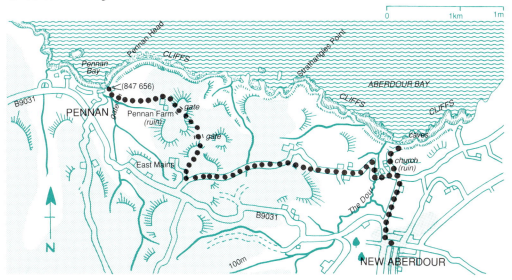

The cliffs only occasionally relent along the coast of Banff and Buchan, but wherever they do there is a harbour. Pennan is one such, and has the charm of its neighbours, Gardenstown and Crovie *(6)*. Pennan is 10 miles east of Macduff on the B9031. A narrow road drops down the steep hill from the main road to the village.

The path starts at the east end of Pennan, behind the harbour. There is a sign indicating a right of way to New Aberdour.

Follow the path which climbs up the hill to the east of a steep, red, sandstone gully, cutting into the fields behind the town. After a short distance there is a gate. Go through this, and continue through the field beyond, walking close to the fence on the right. At the top of the field is the ruined Pennan Farm. Leave the farm to the right and continue. There are two further junctions (stay left at both), after which the route is

straightforward. Along most of the route – between fields the whole way – there are views of the sea and cliff scenery to east and west. After three miles the track joins a narrow road. Half a mile along the road to the right is New Aberdour, a small planned village, founded in 1798 by William Gordon of Aberdour.

Alternatively, a short distance along the road to the left is the ruined mediaeval church of Aberdour; founded by St Columba and dedicated to St Drostan. Beyond the church the road continues down to the sandy Aberdour Beach. Behind the beach is a well, associated by some with St Drostan, while beyond the eastern end of the beach there are some excellent caves cut into the sandstone cliffs.

8 Keith

Length: 2½ miles (4km) from town centre
Height climbed: Negligible
Grade: C
Public conveniences: Keith
Public transport: Bus and railway services
between Aberdeen and Inverness

*A short walk through mixed woodland,
leading to a small waterfall.*

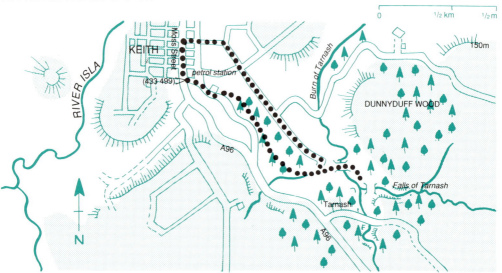

Keith is a neat, sizeable town, situated on the
River Isla (a tributary of the Deveron) in the belt
of rolling, hilly farmland between the coastal plain
by the Moray Firth and the Grampians to the
south.

The town has existed in some form for
centuries but it was not until the 18th and early
19th centuries – the great era for land
improvement – that it became an important local
centre. Keith was indebted to not one benefactor
but two. The main body of the town, laid out in
the grid-iron pattern generally adopted at the time,
was built for the Earl of Findlater in 1750; while,
across the River Isla, the Earl of Fife planned 'Fife
Keith' in 1817. The town's people were employed
in linen and tobacco processing, and the
production of woollen goods and whisky.

To the east of the town the Burn of Tarnash
flows into the Isla. There is a pleasant walk
through the wooded den of the burn to the south of
the town, leading to a small waterfall.

Walk south from the centre of the town along
Moss Street (A96) and turn left after the petrol
station at the edge of the town. When this road
starts to cut up to the left, keep straight on. After a
short distance there is a signpost: 'Den Walk and
Falls of Tarnash'. Walk in the direction indicated,
through a wood of mature broad-leaved and
coniferous trees.

After a little over half a mile the path splits
and a small meadow opens up to the right. Cut
right to reach the falls, overhung by trees in a
rocky, narrow gorge.

Retrace your steps from the falls to the split
in the path. Cut right for an alternative route back
to the centre of Keith.

9 Craigellachie to Dufftown

Length: 6 miles (10km) one way
Height climbed: 270ft (100m)
Grade: B
Public conveniences: Craigellachie and Dufftown
Public transport: Bus service between Dufftown and Elgin, passes Craigellachie

A long, level walk along an old railway route. Path good.

In years gone by there was a rail connection between Elgin and Dufftown. Part of the old line has been used to create a six mile path, cutting east off the Speyside Way, from Craigellachie, at the junction of the Spey and the Fiddich, up Glen Fiddich to Dufftown.

As 'Glen Fiddich' may suggest, this walk runs through the heart of Speyside's Malt whisky area. Apart from the Glenfiddich Distillery in Dufftown (open to the public), there are many others within a short distance of the route, plus coopers and other ancillary industries in both towns.

The best way to walk this route is to take the bus from one end of the route to the other and then walk back.

Craigellachie is a small, pleasant village on the edge of the Spey Valley, famous for its single-span, iron bridge, built by Thomas Telford in 1815. Head east from the town along the A95 road towards Keith. Cut off the road, just before it crosses the Fiddich, into Fiddich Park. From the park the route is signposted as part of the Speyside Way.

The path is clear and there are good views down to the rushing river but the route is somewhat overshadowed by the surrounding trees. The walk is at its best when they are not in full leaf. However, much of the surrounding woodland is very fine and there are some excellent beech, oak, gean and others.

The track joins the A941 and continues along a pavement, past Glenfiddich Distillery and on to Dufftown. As the road passes the distillery, the B9014 cuts off to the left. A short distance down this road is the ruin of Balvenie Castle: first built in the 13th century but with many subsequent additions.

10 Aberlour

Length: 2 miles (3km)
Height climbed: 100ft (30m)
Grade: C
Public conveniences: Aberlour
Public transport: Bus service between Elgin and Dufftown

A short walk through a small, wooded glen on good paths and public roads.

Aberlour is a pleasant town on the banks of the River Spey, with a long, wide main street and a small square. Its full name is 'Charlestown of Aberlour', after Charles Grant, who planned the village in 1812. This is the heart of Malt Whisky country, and there are a number of famous distilleries in the area, some of which – like the Aberlour-Glenlivet Distillery which is passed along this route – are open to the public.

Start walking from the square, down towards the River Spey, leaving the church to your right. The path crosses an area of open parkland by the river and then cuts left, along the riverside. The suspension bridge across the river forms part of the Speyside Way.

When the path reaches the Burn of Aberlour turn left up the near side of the wooded burn. There are three bridges over the Lour below the road – two footbridges and a semi-ruined, single-span bridge. Ignore these and keep straight-on, up to the A95. Cross the road and continue up the path beyond.

Just above the road, on the far side of the burn, is the distillery. A moment's respite and deep inhalation is heavily recommended at this point on the route.

As the path continues, broad-leaved woodland gradually gives way to Scots pine and Douglas fir, and the glen becomes narrower. Half a mile from the road the falls are reached at a bend in the burn, overhung by trees.

Carry straight on, up the steps beside the fall pool, and double back, a short way beyond, on a path through mature conifer woodland. This eventually joins a clearer track, blends into a minor road and winds down into the town.

11 Giant's Chair

Length: 2 ¹/₂ miles (4km)
Height climbed: Negligible
Grade: C
Public conveniences: Dufftown
Public transport: Bus service from Elgin

A short walk through a wooded glen. Back by a quiet public road.

Dufftown, at the confluence of the Dullan Water and the Fiddich, is at the heart of Speyside's Malt Whisky industry. It is the home of the famous Glenfiddich Distillery, as well as a number of others; two of which are passed on this walk.

The town was laid out in 1817 by the 4th Earl of Fife, but the site had earlier, religious associations – particularly with St Moluag of Lismore, who founded the church of Mortlach in AD 566.

To start the walk, follow the road signs from the centre of Dufftown for Kirkton of Mortlach. Enter into the church grounds. Parts of the building are thought to date from the 12th century. Walk down through the churchyard to the Dullan Water and cross over the footbridge to the new cemetery. Turn right along the river bank.

A short distance along the path the Dufftown-Glenlivet distillery comes into view to the right, with barrels stacked in the yard by the riverside and powerful fumes wafting across the water.

The route is quite clear; continuing up the side of the glen. This becomes increasingly narrow and wooded until, eventually, the path has to climb up from the water side, crossing two small tributaries. A short way beyond these is the 'Giant's Chair' – a water-scooped hollow in the lip of a small cliff above the burn – beyond which the path crosses the Dullan by a footbridge, continues across the small meadow beyond, and then climbs up to the public road. Turn right to return to Dufftown.

As the road nears Mortlach it passes the Dufftown-and neighbouring Pittyvaich-Glenlivet Distilleries.

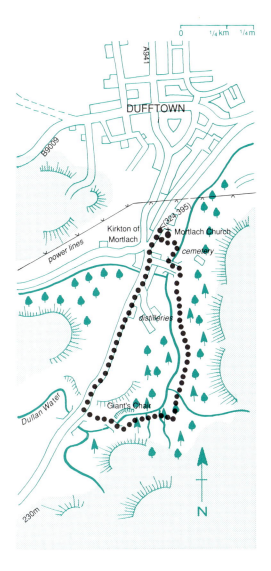

12 Ben Rinnes

Length: 6 miles (9.5km) there and back
Height climbed: 1750ft (530m)
Grade: A
Public conveniences: None
Public transport: None

A straight, moorland hill climb. Paths of varying quality. Views excellent.

Ben Rinnes is one of the most distinctive of Scottish hills, due to the three 'scurrans' – corrugated and split granite outcrops or 'tors' – at the summit.

The hill sits five miles south-west of Dufftown, between the River Spey and the Dullan Water. The views from the summit are excellent.

To reach the walk, drive south from Dufftown on the B9009 for four miles, and then turn right on the unnumbered road to Edinvillie. After half a mile a gate appears in a fence to the left. This is the start of the walk. Parking is very restricted but there are one or two places near the gate where a car can be parked off the road.

The early part of the track is very clear but it becomes less so on some sections of the hill. There should be no problem with the route, however; simply climb over the 'steps' of Round Hill and Roy's Hill, and then continue up the hill's

pronounced eastern buttress to the easterly Scurran of Lochterlandoch. The path can be damp on the lower steps, and the angled plateau at the top is also liable to be marshy, but it is not difficult to cross to the two westerly scurrans, across the pitted landscape of peat hags and mosses.

The scurrans provide plenty of cover at the top, and there are excellent views in all directions: north, across the hills of Meikle and Little Conval to the Moray Firth; east to the rolling hill land around Glen Fiddich; and south to the Cairngorms. Even when the weather is damp and the views restricted, there is still the warming thought that the rain which falls help to fill the countless stills in the surrounding glens.

13 Tomintoul Country Walk

Length: 5 1/2 miles (9km) from town centre
Height climbed: Undulating
Grade: B
Public conveniences: Tomintoul
Public transport: Occasional bus service from
Grantown, Ballater and Elgin; check locally

*A short walk on good tracks and metalled
roads through farmland, woodland and
moorland in a high valley.*

Tomintoul is a long, thin town, founded in 1779
by the 4th Duke of Gordon. At 1160ft/350m
above sea level it can lay claim to being the
highest village in the Scottish Highlands. A more
relevant fact for walker is that it is the first town
to the north-east of the Cairngorms; placed where
the last of the farmland of the North East gives
way to high peaks and moorland. The river to the
west of the town is the Avon, which gathers its
head-waters from the flanks of Ben Macdhui and
Cairn Gorm. This walk follows the valley of the
Avon.

To start the walk go to the southern end of the
town and follow the signs for 'Delnabo'. From
this road there are views across fields and down
Strath Avon to the Hills of Cromdale to the north-
west.

Half a mile from Tomintoul, just beyond a
white cottage, the road splits. There is parking up
the track to the left. Carry on walking to the right,
across the bridge over the wide, shallow, fast-
flowing Avon, and on, along a metalled road by
the Water of Ailnack, to the house at Delnabo.
The road is flanked by fields at this point and the
surroundings are more pastoral than might be
expected.

The road cuts left across the Ailnack and
continues up the main valley. After half a mile it
becomes a private road and is only open to
walkers. A further half a mile on, having passed
through an area of scrub woodland, the track splits
again, at the farm of Delavorar. Cut left, across the
Avon, and then left again, down a clear track back
to the road. A feature of the east side of the glen
are the large stands of juniper amongst the birch
trees.

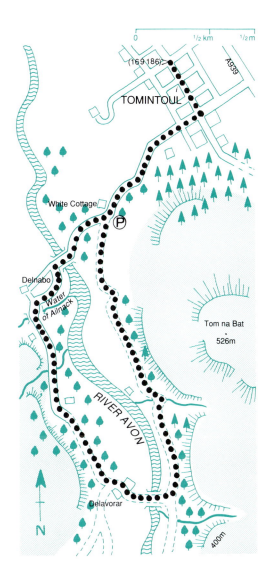

14 Bennachie

Length: Any distance
Height climbed: Up to 1300ft (400m);undulating
Grade: A/B/C
Public conveniences: Car parks
Public transport: None

A number of paths of varying lengths through forestry and across high moorland, leading to excellent views from hill peaks.

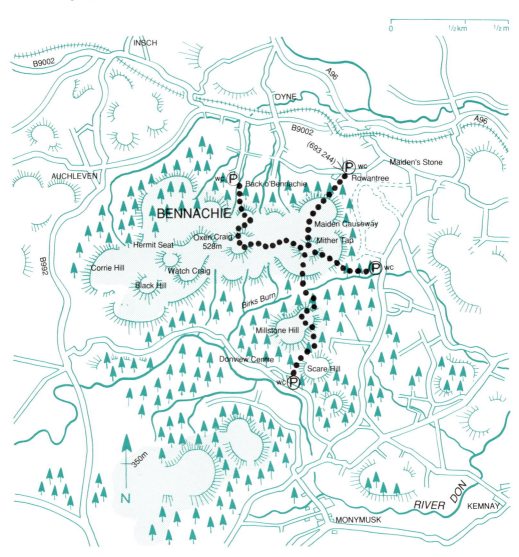

Walk 14

Bennachie is one of the most distinctive landmarks in the North East. Fifteen miles north-west of Aberdeen it rises from the low, rolling farmland: the last eastwards peak of the northern Grampians. The hill has a distinctive shape, its summit being punctuated with rocky tors. The most obvious of these is the Mither Tap, at the eastern end of the summit plateau.

Bennachie is a granite hill; draped in forestry about its lower slopes, and thick with heather about the tops. As with all Scottish hills, it was once much higher but was ground down by the glaciers of the ice age. The tors are formed of harder rock-types which proved more resistant to the ice.

The hill is now one of the most popular walking areas in the North East. A number of forest walks are maintained in the plantations around the car parks and there are longer hill walks across the moorland between the tops. There are four car parks around the hill, and they are interconnected by the footpaths. These car parks are all reached through the tangle of unnumbered, narrow roads to the south of the A96 Aberdeen to Inverness road, just to the west of Inverurie. The car parks are signposted, and the roads – too complicated to describe – are shown on the map over the page.

Similarly, there are far too many possible walks on the hill to describe them all in detail here. The main paths are shown overleaf, while the shorter, forest walks are illustrated on signposts in the car parks. All the paths are signposted along their routes.

There are a number of interesting points on Bennachie. Perhaps the most impressive is the fort at Mither Tap. At its eastern end the hill rises sharply to a point, and is topped by the most extravagant of the tors: a mass of granite blocks, scarred and chiselled along their weakest points, and with edges smoothed by the ice. At some time the path leading up to the tor from the Rowantree car park was built up and roughly paved (probably by the fort-builders, around the time of the birth of Christ), and the tor itself surrounded by a great stone rampart, the stones of which still lie in a disordered ring around its base.

Four miles to the east of Mither Tap is the site of the Battle of Harlaw (1411), fought between the Lord of the Isles and the Earl of Mar during the former's campaign to win the Earldom of Ross. By the side of the Maiden's Causeway there is a memorial of the battle, at 'Hessie's Well'. This marks the burial place of a man who was called to the battle to help repulse the Highlanders on the eve of his wedding. During the Highlanders' retreat he was captured, and was subsequently imprisoned on the Hebrides for some years. On returning he discovered that his true love had married another, and died of a broken heart. Or so they say.

A somewhat older monument sits by the road a little to the east of the Rowantree car park. The Maiden's Stone is a carved, Pictish symbol stone of the 8th or 9th century, about 11ft/3.5m high, and covered with a mixture of Christian and traditional Pictish symbols.

Much of the hill is now owned by the Forestry Commission, and most of the woodland on the lower slopes is grown for commercial purposes. The trees planted include Scots pine, lodgepole pine, larch, spruce and Douglas fir.

On the upper slopes the moorland is clear, the walking fine and the views excellent. On the top of Mither Tap there is a view indicator.

15 Tap o'Noth

Length: 4 miles (6.5km) there and back
Height climbed: 1050ft (320m)
Grade: B
Public conveniences: Rhynie
Public transport: Bus services from Aberdeen
and Huntly

*A short hill climb across moorland on a good
track, leading to an iron-age fort. Views
excellent.*

As the Grampians peter out towards the north east,
into a lumpy landscape of farmland and moorland,
the conical peak and long ridge of Tap o'Noth
rises to the west of the valley of the Water of
Bogie; two miles north-west of the town of
Rhynie.

Rhynie is a small, pleasant, airy village, set
in a deep valley created by the erosion of a band
of sandstone. At the southern end of the village is
the Old Kirkyard, with its two early examples of
Pictish symbol stones.

To reach Rhynie drive eight miles south from
Huntly on the A97.

For this walk, drive a further two miles east
of Rhynie on the A941 (the Dufftown road) and
then turn right on to the minor road signposted for
'Milton of Lesmore' and park.

Start walking up the road beyond the farm at
Milton of Lesmore. When the path splits, keep

right; through a gate and on, up, across a slope
with a small conifer plantation to the left. After the
track crosses a small burn cut right, across a field,
through a gate at the top of the field and on, up to
the edge of a forestry plantation. From the top of
the plantation the track is clear; up across the
moorland to the summit.

At the top are the remains of a fort: a huge
stone rampart enclosing an area of some 300 sq m.
Parts of the wall are vitrified: the stones fused by
the heat of a great fire, probably at the time of the
fort's destruction.

Either return by the same route or walk north,
over the Hill of Noth and down the Glen of Noth,
to join the A97, three miles north of Rhynie.

16 Sands of Forvie

Length: Up to 8 miles (13km)
Height climbed: Undulating
Grade: B
Public conveniences: Collieston
Public transport: Bus from Aberdeen, stops at junction of B9003 and A975.

A number of paths through a large area of sand dunes edged by cliffs.

The River Ythan flows east from the hills of Strathbogie and meets the North Sea in a wide, muddy estuary, some 10 miles north of the edge of Aberdeen. The Ythan estuary is famous for its fishing and its rich bird-life and for the wide area of shifting sand dunes to the north of the river: the Sands of Forvie.

To reach the sands drive north from Aberdeen on the A92, turning right onto the A975, and then right again – some two miles after crossing the Ythan – on to the B9003 to Collieston: a pleasant old harbour village.

Before Collieston is reached a road cuts right, signposted to the Forvie Wildlife Education Centre. The sands are now a National Nature Reserve and information on local wildlife is available at the centre. Forvie Sands is one of the largest areas of dunes in Britain, and the reserve includes both fixed and mobile dunes, cliffs and sandy moorland, plus all the associated wildlife.

Start walking from the centre, along the indicated paths; winding south through lumpy, heath covered dunes, dotted with occasional small lochs, towards the cliffs-top path along the coast. A little over two miles from the centre are the ruins of Forvie Kirk. The church was built in 704 and at one time was surrounded by a mediaeval village. This had to be abandoned in 1413 due to the encroachment of the sands.

Follow the track beyond, down to the Ythan, and turn left along the estuary towards the bright red/brown dunes by the river mouth. Cut left before these (the peninsula is cordoned off for breeding terns) and cross the neck of the peninsula to the beach beyond. Turn left to return to Forvie Kirk.

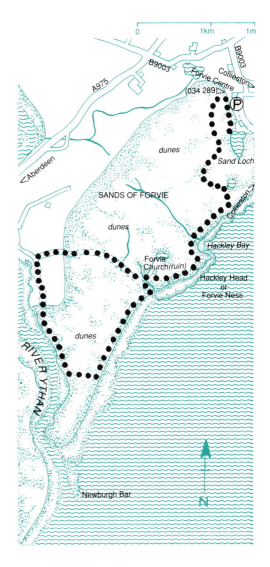

17 Forest Walks

The map below shows the locations of seven forest walks. All the routes are comparatively short and simple and all are suitable for dogs. There are public conveniences at routes 1, 4, 5 and 7.

None of these routes can be reached by public transport.

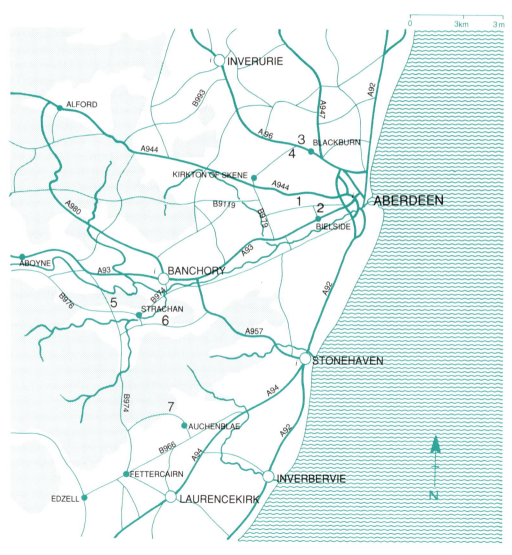

The Forestry Commission have created a number of walks through their plantations in the North East, some of which are noted below. The whereabouts of each route can be checked on the map on the previous page, while more detailed descriptions of each route can be found in a Forestry Commission publication called 'Forest Walks in Aberdeen Area', which is available locally from tourist information offices. In addition, all of these routes are signposted and can be followed without the use of a map.

1) Countesswells Wood

Directions: Drive four miles west from Aberdeen city centre to Bieldside, on the A93 Banchory road, and turn right onto the minor road signposted for Blacktop. When the road reaches a T junction either turn left for one mile (Rotten of Gairn car park), or right, then first left (Loanhead car park).

Walks: Four routes, from 1-2 miles (2-3km)

2) Foggieton

Directions: Drive four miles west from Aberdeen city centre to Bieldside, on the A93 Banchory road, and turn right onto the minor road signposted for Blacktop. The car park is a little over a mile along this road.

Walks: Three routes, from $1/2$-1mile (1-2km), largely through broad-leaved woodland.

3) Tyrebagger Wood

Directions: Drive seven miles north west from Aberdeen city centre on the A96 Inverness road. Turn right two miles after Bankhead and follow the signs for the 'Wayfaring Course'. The car park is just off the main road.

Walks: Three routes, from 3-4 miles (4.5-6km), largely through conifers.

4) Saplinbrae and Glendale

Directions: Drive seven miles north west from Aberdeen city centre on the A96 Inverness road, and turn left onto the B979 road to Kirkton of Skene. The car park is a short distance along this road to the left.

Walks: Three routes, from $3/4$-$1 1/2$ miles (1-2km), largely through conifers. In addition, there are further paths across the open top of Elrick Hill, to the south, which are joined to the main paths.

5) Blackhall

Directions: Drive south from Banchory on the B974 road to Strachan, then cut onto the B976 towards Aboyne. Two miles from Strachan cut right onto the narrow road signposted for the forest walks. The car park is $1 1/2$ miles up this road.

Walks: Three routes, from 1-3 miles (1.6-4.8km), largely through conifer plantations.

6) Mulloch

Directions: Follow the B974 road south from Banchory to Strachan, and on across the Water of Feugh; then take the first turn to the left, onto a minor road. The car park is three miles along this road.

Walks: One walk of $2 1/2$ miles (3.9km), providing some good views of Deeside, plus the Nine Stones circle of standing stones, surrounding an inner burial chamber.

7) Drumtochty

Directions: Drive eight miles south of Stonehaven on the A94, then turn right on the road signposted to Auchenblae. Follow the minor road north from Auchenblae – which ultimately joins the B974 Banchory to Fettercairn road – for two miles, to the car park in the Glen of Drumtochty.

Walks: One walk of 1 mile (1.5km), largely through conifers.

18 Morrone

Length: 4 miles (6.5km)
Height climbed: 1600ft (490m)
Grade: B
Public conveniences: Braemar
Public transport: Bus service up Deeside from Aberdeen

A brisk hill climb, through birch woods and across moorland, leading to fine views. Paths rough.

From Auchendryne (the western side of Braemar) follow Chapel Brae out of the edge of the village. To the left of the road there is a car park by a lochan.

Follow the track which continues beyond and, when the path splits, keep left. The route winds gently uphill through the birch and juniper of the Morrone Birch Wood Nature Reserve. Sections of the wood are fenced off to encourage regeneration. After about ¼ mile the path splits once again. Keep to the left once more. An indicator has been erected near the split and there is a fine view of the surrounding hills.

A short distance along the clear track beyond, and a little before it passes the ruin at Tomintoul, there is a cairn on the hillside to the right. Turn up the hill at this point. At first the path is not clear but the route is marked by a series of cairns.

At the summit of the hill there is an Aberdeen University laboratory and wireless mast. The views of the surrounding hills are excellent *(see below)*.

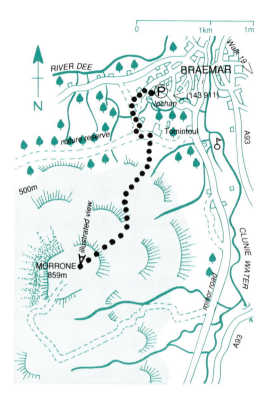

1. Ben Avon (1171m) 2. Culdaroch (900m) 3. Creag Choinnich (538m) 4. Morven (871m)
5. Lochnagar (1155m) 6. Loch Callater 7. Carn an Tuirc (1019m)

19 Creag Choinnich

Length: Up to 4 miles (6.5km)
Height climbed: 700ft (210m)
Grade: B/C
Public conveniences: Braemar
Public transport: Bus service up Deeside from
Aberdeen

*A series of paths through the woods to the
east of Braemar, including a short climb to
fine views from Creag Choinnich.*

Braemar is a small town, 1100ft/335m above sea
level, in the upper part of Deeside. It is comprised
of two smaller villages: Auchendryne and
Castleton, lying to the west and east, respectively,
of the Clunie Water, as it nears the River Dee. The
castle in Castleton was Kindrochit *(bridge-end)*.
Originally built in the 14th century by Malcolm de
Drummond, it became a fortress of great
importance but is now reduced to a few crumbling
walls, situated by the Tourist Information Centre.
The town is now best known for its annual
Highland Games, which are held each September
in the presence of the Royal Family.

To the east of Braemar is the bald head of
Creag Choinnich, rising above a forest of conifers.
There are a number of paths through the forest,
including a track to the summit of the hill.

From the centre of the town walk south along
Glen Shee Road; turning left at the signpost for

the walk. After a short distance along this new
road cut left through a gate into open Scots pine
and larch woodland. The paths are clear, and the
various routes are colour-coded and signposted at
each junction.

The path up Creag Choinnich climbs through
a band of close-planted forestry before breaking
out onto steep moorland. The path to the summit is
rough but not difficult. At the top there is a large
cairn from which there are fine views in all
directions: north-west to the mass of Beinn
a'Bhuird, down to Braemar and on up Glen Dee,
south up Glen Clunie, and east down Deeside.
Across the valley is Invercauld House and, from
the northern edge of the hill, there is a fine view
down to Braemar Castle at the foot of the hill.

20 Craigendarroch

Length: 2 miles (3km)
Height climbed: 650ft (200m)
Grade: C
Public conveniences: Ballater
Public transport: Bus service up Deeside from Aberdeen

A short hill climb through mature, mixed woodland. Excellent views.

Ballater lies in a crook of the River Dee. There was an inn on the site in the late 18th century but the town did not grow substantially until Queen Victoria and Prince Albert bought Balmoral Castle, seven miles to the west, and the area became fashionable for holidays; a fashion made possible by the advent of the Deeside railway (now closed).

Behind Ballater is Craigendarroch *(The Hill of the Oaks)*; a rounded, tree-covered, granite mound jutting out into the valley.

To reach the hill, walk out from the centre of the town along the A93, towards Braemar. Turn right up 'Craigendarroch Walk'. This road leads to the foot of the hill.

There are a number of paths through the wood but the two main tracks – one around the hill and one to the summit – are signposted. The south side of the hill is covered in mature oakwood, while the damper, cooler, north side has a cover of Scots pine, larch, birch, rowan, etc. The trees extend almost to the summit, but the top is rocky and clear, with a cairn of grey and pink granite. The views are unobstructed and excellent.

1. Craig Coillich (397m) 2. Pannanich Hill (601m) 3. Mount Keen (939m) 4. Glen Muick House
5. Cairn Leuchan (699m) 6. The Coyle (596m) 7. Conachcraig (865m)

21 Loch Muick

Length: 8 miles (13km)
Height climbed: Negligible
Grade: A
Public conveniences: Spittal of Glen Muick
Public transport: None

*A long walk, on generally good paths, around
a large inland loch in a steep, narrow glen.*

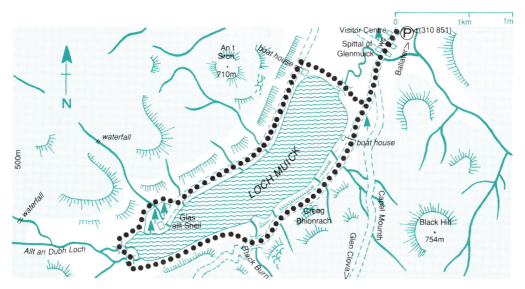

Glen Muick *(Glen of the Pig)* leads deep into the
wild hill land south of Deeside; and Loch Muick,
at its head, sits at the foot of the buttresses of
Lochnagar, to the west.

To reach the loch, cross the River Dee at
Ballater, turn right for half a mile, and then left,
up the glen. It is eight miles to the Spittal of
Glenmuick car park, where red deer are fed by the
warden of the Nature Reserve.

Start walking along the path beyond the car
park. In a stand of trees there is a small visitor
centre, listing some of the plants, birds and
animals which may be seen in the area. Just
beyond this, a track cuts off to the right. This is
part of the Lochnagar path and also of a short,
three mile, walk by Allt-na-giubhsaich *(Burn of
the Firs)*.

Half a mile further on a track cuts up to the
left. This is the start of the Capel Mounth path to

Glen Clova. Carry straight on, to reach the edge of
Loch Muick.

The path is wide and clear until it reaches the
bridge over the Black Burn, about half way down
the loch. Once over the bridge cut right, off the
main track and on to a rougher path which winds
along the steep slope above the loch. The waterfall
of Allt Loch Buidhe *(Burn of the Yellow Loch)* is
visible ahead.

At the head of the loch there are two bridges
across the meandering waters of Allt an Dubh
Loch. Beyond these, the path skirts around the
loch to the pine and larch wood around the grey
granite lodge of Glas Allt Sheil. Cut left and follow
the edge of the wood until it rejoins the track –
clear and flat once again – beyond the lodge.

Turn right at the boathouse at the foot of the
loch to rejoin the original track.

Walk 21

22 Glen Tanar √

Length: 4 miles (6.5km)
Height climbed: Negligible
Grade: B
Public conveniences: Visitor centre
Public transport: None

Three routes of varying lengths through farm-land, forestry and natural pine woodland. Paths good.

Perhaps the most distinctive feature of Deeside are the Scots pine trees, which are planted in great numbers throughout much of the valley. In Glen Tanar – a tributary glen to the south of Deeside – there are three walks laid out, the longest of which leads to a fine plantation to those noble trees.

To reach Glen Tanar, turn off the B976 at Bridge o'Ess between Dinnet and Aboyne on the south side of the River Dee. The car park is two miles up the glen on the right-hand side; and a footbridge across the river leads to the visitor's centre at Braeloine. At the centre there is information about the various land uses throughout the Glen Tanar Estate.

The three routes through the glen are signposted and colour-coded. They all start along the track up the Water of Tanar. The longest leads out across farmland, past the little chapel of Lesmo (built 1872), and then cuts through a stand of commercial forestry. At the far end of the forestry a track leads off to the left; this is the start of the Firmounth Road, leading over the hills to the south to Glen Esk. A short distance to the right is a viewpoint with an annotated sketch explaining the reasons and uses for the surrounding forestry. Beyond this the path doubles back to the riverside and then cuts hard left up the river, passing through a mile of Scots pine woodland – a type of ground cover once common throughout most of the Highlands, but now restricted to a few scattered patches, notably in Deeside and Speyside – to a wooden footbridge over the river, and then doubling back down the far side; recrossing the Tanar a little before Glen Tanar House and returning to Braeloine by the riverside.

23 Scolty Hill ✓

Length: 5 miles (8km)
Height climbed: 800ft (250m)
Grade: B
Public conveniences: Banchory
Public transport: Bus service along Deeside
from Aberdeen

*A short, steep hill climb; through conifers
and across moorland. Fine views.*

Banchory is a busy, prosperous town on the River
Dee, some 18 miles west of Aberdeen on the
A93. to the south of the town, across the river,
the northern hills of the Mounth – the eastern spur
of the Grampians – run up to the river's edge.

To the south-west of the town is the heathery
peak of Scolty Hill, rising above the surrounding
forestry in the fork made by the glens of the Dee
and the Water of Feugh. The hill is crowned by a
tall tower.

To reach the hill, walk south from the town
centre, along Dee Street, and cross the bridge
over the wide, shallow river. Climb up the steps
beyond the bridge and then cut right along a
minor road between fields and a high wall. From
the steps onwards the walk is signposted: along
the road, through a wood of commercial conifers
interspersed with birch and beech, and up, across
a stretch of steep moorland, to the summit.

The views from the top are very fine: south
and west across Glen Feugh to the Mounth; north
to the Hill of Fare and east towards Aberdeen and
the North Sea.

HILL OF FARE

1. Craigrath (436m) 2. Grey More (393m) 3. Meikle Tap (359m) 4. Crathes Gardens 5. River Dee

24 Dunnottar ✓

Length: 3 miles (5km)
Height climbed: 250ft (70m) undulating
Grade: C
Public conveniences: Stonehaven
Public transport: Bus and train services to
Stonehaven from all directions

*A coastal walk along cliff tops; passing a fine
ruined castle.*

Few Scottish ruins have the position, grandeur and
blood-stained history of Dunnottar; perched on its
cliff-edged rocky outcrop, jutting out into the
North Sea.

It is not known when the rock was first
fortified, but a fort is mentioned as early as the
13th century, and such a prime defensive site must
surely have been fortified long before that. The
present building was begun in the late 14th
century by Sir William Keith. Additions continued
to be made up until the late 17th century.

The castle's fine situation ensured that it
played a central role in the wars of Scotland; most
particularly during the Wars of the Covenant in
the 17th century. It was beseiged unsuccessfully in
1645 by Montrose, for Charles I, and successfully
in 1651-52 by General Overton, for Cromwell. In
1685 the castle was used as a prison for
covenanting prisoners during Argyll's rebellion. A
number of them died while trying to escape down
the sheer cliffs to the north of the castle.

Follow the minor road, south from
Stonehaven, and park in the castle car park. Take
the path towards the castle but turn left, along the
cliff-top, before reaching it; along the top of the
grassy cliffs. The way is clear but rough. **Great
care should be taken as this path runs close to
the cliff-edge.**

After a little under a mile there is a
prominent war memorial on a hill to the left of the
path, from where there are fine views: south to
Dunnottar; north to Stonehaven and beyond;
eastwards out to the North Sea.

From the memorial, either turn back along
the same route or continue on the path until it
reaches the road and then turn left, along the
pavement and back to the car park.

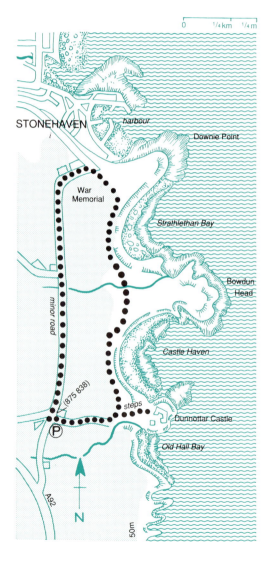

Walk 24

25 Glen Esk

Length: 5 miles (8km)
Height climbed: 650ft (220m)
Grade: B
Public conveniences: None
Public transport: None

A short moorland hill walk on rough tracks; leading to fine views of the surrounding hills.

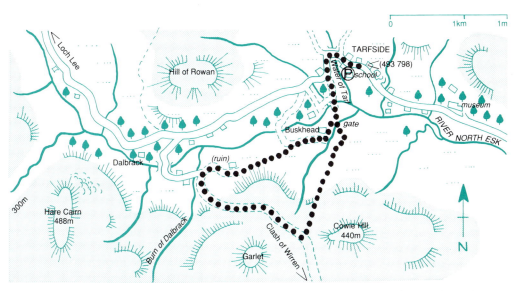

The headwaters of the River North Esk are gathered in the hills on the northern boundary of Angus, and the river then flows south-east, crossing the Highland Line at the falls behind Edzell *(26)*. Glen Esk surrounds the section of the river north of the Highland Line. To reach the glen turn onto an unnumbered road off the B966 Edzell to Fettercairn road, 1 1/2 miles north of Edzell. Some 12 miles up the glen is the tiny village of Tarfside.

Park in the car park – to the left of the road, beyond the school – and walk on along the road, across the Water of Tarf to a junction. Cut left (signposted 'Loch Lee') for a short distance and then, opposite a small cottage, cut left again, off the road, through a gate, and follow the track beyond to the bridge over the river. At this point the valley bottom is full of scattered birch trees, clustered on lumpy moraines.

Cross the river and continue up the track towards Buskhead Farm. Just before the farm the path splits. Cut left, and then, almost immediately, right, through a gate, and on up the vague, grassy track through the moorland above.

The path leads up to the saddle between Garlet and Cowie Hill, from where there are splendid views of the hills around the head of the glen, and of the path cutting south, around East Knock, to the Clash of Wirren and Glen Lethnot beyond.

Drop north-west, along a clear track, to join the track east of Dalbrack. Cut right, past the ruin of Drumgreen, and on. The path disappers for a spell – continue along the flood plain and it eventually reappears, passes Buskhead and rejoins the original track.

26 Edzell

Length: 7½ miles (12km)
Height climbed: 150ft (40m)
Grade: B
Public conveniences: Edzell
Public transport: Buses from Brechin and
Montrose

*A riverside path through mixed woodland,
starting in low farmland and climbing to the
edge of the Angus Hills.*

Edzell is a small, airy town, situated in the flat
farmland of Strathmore, six miles north of Brechin
on the B966.

This walk follows rough paths through the
woodland by the River North Esk. At first the
river flows through farmland, and the woods are
predominantly of mature beech, but in the upper
section of the path the glen becomes more
'Highland', and the tree cover changes to Scots
pine, larch, birch, rowan and alder.

To start the walk cut east off the main street,
following the sign beside the Post Office
indicating the way 'To Riverside and Shakkin'
Brig'. Follow the track down to the river and then
cut left. After a short distance a suspension bridge
crosses the river to the right, while the path
continues through the woods on the west bank.

The river is broad, shallow and swift at this
stage, and the banks are low. Gradually, however,
they become higher and steeper until, 1½ miles
north of Edzell, as the path nears the B966, there
is a deep gorge; mossy and overhung with trees.

Cross a stile onto the road and cut right
across the bridge; then left, through a small gate,
onto the path through the upper glen.

A short way above the bridge the river
crosses the Highland Boundary Fault. The
disruption of the rocks around this line has created
some spectacular falls and rapids.

The path continues for a further 1½
dramatic miles before joining the public road up
Glen Esk. Either return by the same path, or cut
right, down the road. If the latter, then turn left at
the junction with the B966, then first right towards
'RAF Edzell'. After one mile turn right on a rough
track, leading back to Edzell across the Shakkin'
Brig.

Walk 26

27 Caterthuns

Length: 2 miles (3km)
Height climbed: White: 250ft (70m);
Brown: 200ft (60m)
Grade: C
Public conveniences: None
Public transport: None

*Two short climbs on rough tracks to two
ancient hill forts. Excellent views.*

The Brown and White Caterthuns are hill forts,
perched on the peaks of two low, round hills near
the Highland Line, on the north side of
Strathmore. To reach the forts from Brechin,
follow the minor road north to Little Brechin, and
then continue along the road towards Kirkton of
Memnmuir. Once on this road carry sraight on for
three miles, turning neither right nor left at the
next three junctions, to reach the car park.

From Edzell, follow the signs fro Kirriemuir
and Menmuir and turn right at the sign for the
Caterthuns. The car park is at the high point of a
narrow road, between the two hills.

The Brown Caterthun, to the east, is the
older, and less impressive of the two forts. The
path runs to the left of a fence, through heather
moorland. The fort was built in the late pre-
Christian era, and now comprises a series of
concentric mounds. The views are excellent: west
to the hills of Angus; south-east across the
farmland of Strathmore to Montrose Basin.

The path to the White Caterthun is shorter
and clearer. To the left of the path is an open
woodland of Scots pine, larch and spruce.

The fort was built in the early Christian
period by the Picts, or their immediate ancestors.
Its main feature is a large oval dyke of pink and
grey granite enclosing an area of some 500x220ft.
Outside this wall there are further, small ramparts.
The views are, once again, excellent.

Return by the same route.

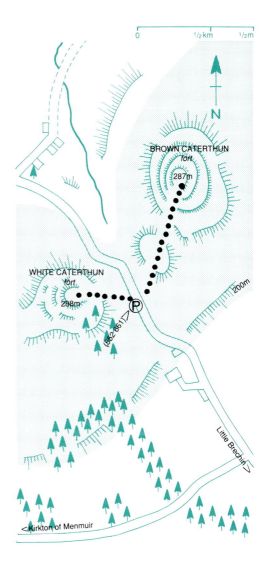

28 St Cyrus

Length: 3 ½ miles (5.5km)
Height climbed: 200ft (60m)
Grade: C
Public conveniences: St Cyrus
Public transport: Bus service from Montrose

A short walk; along sand beaches, dunes and low cliffs. The area is a Nature Reserve.

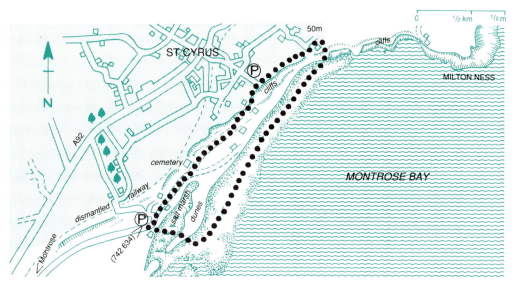

The village of St Cyrus sits slightly inland, by the A92; five miles north of Montrose. To the east are the low, grassy cliffs, sand dunes, salt marshes and wide sands of St Cyrus Nature Reserve.

There is a car park on the cliff edge, directly to the east of the village, and another at the south end of the beach. To reach the latter, drive one mile south of St Cyrus along the main road, and turn left down a narrow road, immediately after passing a narrow belt of trees. This road winds dramatically down the steep slope to the shore.

This is more a place to wander than a specific route, but there is a path: north, through the dunes, past the salt marsh, the old cemetery and the whitewashed buildings and drying nets of the salmon fishermen. After a little under a mile cut left on a steep path up the face of the basalt cliffs to the St Cyrus car park and continue along the cliff-top; joining a narrow road which runs past

the farm by the cliff-edge, and doubling back down a fine, built-up path along the cliff-face. From the path there are splendid views of the rocky cliffs to the north, the sandy beach and the North Sea. Along the sands there are a number of salmon nets, strung out along high wooden poles down to the foot of the beach.

The Nature Reserve was established to protect a number of sensitive habitats. The basalt cliffs are very fertile, and can support a number of plant species which would not otherwise survive this far north, while the dunes provide a nesting site for terns. As always in such areas, you are asked to disturb the wildlife as little as possible, and to stick to the paths through the dunes.

29 *Montrose Basin*

Length: 3 miles (5km)
Height climbed: Negligible
Grade: C
Public conveniences: Montrose
Public transport: Buses from Montrose along
A935 and A934, to north and south of Basin

*A short walk through grazing land by a
muddy estuary. Fine bird-watching.*

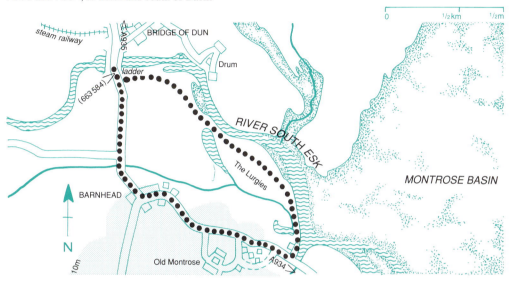

The River North Esk flows south-east down Glen
Clova then cuts east, across Strathmore, to empty
into Montrose Basin, and from there into the sea.

The basin is an area of particular interest to
bird-watchers. It is a muddy tidal estuary, some
two miles square, which is flooded and emptied
twice daily by the tides. Across the shallow
waters, the meandering river and the huge mud
and gravel banks, a host of gulls, geese, ducks,
swans and waders search for food.

The area is now a local nature reserve, and
there is a path which follows the last mile of the
North Esk as it flows down to the edge of the
basin. The path starts at Bridge of Dun.

To reach the start, drive north from the centre
of Montrose on the A92, cut left onto the A935
(while still in the town), and then left again, after
three miles, onto an unnumbered road for a short
distance. There is limited parking by the bridge-
end.

Climb down the short metal ladder from the
bridge and start walking through the meadowland
by the river bank, climbing onto the flood barrier
to the right as the ground becomes damper.

As the path continues along the dyke the view
of the basin, and of the handsome town of Montrose on the far side, gradually opens up. The
path finally leaves the waterside at a tiny harbour.
From the harbour, either return by the same route,
or follow the track up to the public road and
follow it back to the Bridge of Dun. **This road is
very narrow, and care must be taken with
oncoming traffic.**

A short distance from the harbour is Old
Montrose, on the site of the castle from which the
great 17th-century general, James Graham,
Marquess of Montrose, took his title.

30 Ferryden

Length: 5 miles (8km)
Height climbed: Negligible
Grade: B
Public conveniences: Ferryden
Public transport: Bus and train services to
Montrose from Dundee; bus service from Brechin

*A fine coastal walk on rough paths. Back by
quiet public roads.*

Ferryden is a small town on the south side of the
entrance to Montrose Basin. At the western end
of the town ships dock against the harbour walls
downstream from the two bridges across the
basin's exit; at its eastern end the town falls into a
mass of little fishermen's houses.

There is a car park in the middle of the town.
Follow the road above this, eastwards, out of the
town and along the side of a grassy bank above
the inlet. From this road there are fine views:
west to the bridges, the basin and the hills around
the Angus Glens beyond; north to Montrose with
its sandy beach stretching down to the North Sea,
and the lines of the salmon nets stretched across
the sand.

The road goes as far as the lighthouse on
Scurdie Ness. Follow the grassy path around the
outer wall of the buildings and on around the
point. The path winds south around two rocky
bays; both attracting large numbers of eider
ducks. The first bay has a sandy head; while at
the second – below the farm at Mains of Usan –
there are a number of ruined buildings and a little
mausoleum.

The path now continues to Usan – visible on
the horizon – where there is a very small natural
harbour and a few lobster and salmon boats.
Some of the houses are still occupied, but the
main terrace of cottages, with its central clock
tower, is now ruined.

Walk up the quiet public road beyond the
village. At the first junction keep straight on.
Usan House is now visible in the trees to the
right. At the second junction cut right, and at the
next left; then carry on straight ahead, between
fields, back to Ferryden.

31 Minister's Path

Length: 4 miles (6.5km) one way
Height climbed: 550ft (170m)
Grade: A (there and back); B (one way)
Public conveniences: None
Public transport: Bus and postbus services up
the glens from Kirriemuir

A short, lineal hill track; crossing moorland between two parallel glens.

Glen Clova and Glen Prosen are the two central
Glens of Angus. They run south-east from the
hills south of Lochnagar and east of Glas Maol
and cross the Highland Line near Cortachty
Castle. The upper sections of the glens are very
dramatic but there is pleasant walking in the lower
stretches too, including this fine old path over the
hills between the two.

To reach Glen Prosen, follow the B955 north
from Kirriemuir – the road is signposted for the
glens – to Dykehead, then turn left up an
unnumbered road. Near the foot of the glen is a
memorial to Edward Wilson and Captain Scott,
who planned their tragic trip to the South Pole at
Wilson's house in the glen.

Six miles up the glen is Glen Prosen Village.
Park by the church, before the small bridge over
the Burn of Inchmill, and start walking up the
wooded track between the two. Almost
immediately the track splits: stay right, past
Pitcarrity Cottage and out of the trees. The Right
of Way is signposted at this point.

The path starts climbing through grazing land,
with a stand of conifers to the left, but soon
reaches open moorland, where the incline
becomes less steep. The view back across Glen
Prosen is very fine, and the fingers of burnt
moorland – different shades depending on the
number of years since burning – obvious.

The path is rough and damp in places, but
clear; over the watershed, across a small burn, and
down, through a forestry plantation, to the road.
There are fine views on the descent of the peaks
and corries beyond Glen Clova.

Return by the same route.

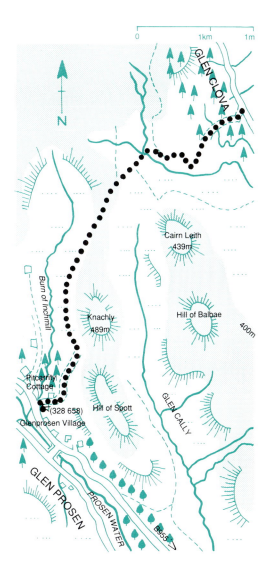

32 Loch Brandy

Length: 5 miles (8km)
Height climbed: 200ft (600m)
Grade: A
Public conveniences: Clova
Public transport: Postbus from Kirriemuir

A steep, short hill walk, leading around the high cliffs surrounding a corrie and a small loch.

Clova is a small group of houses, a school and a hotel, at the head of the B955 road up Glen Clova. To reach the glen follow the signposted road north from Kirriemuir.

The hills are small and gentle by the mouth of the glen but, around Clova, they reach up towards 3000ft/915m, and the slopes become steeper and more marked with rock and scree.

Park in Clova and walk up between the hotel and the school. Beside the latter there is a sign indicating a 'Public Footpath to Glen Esk'. The track starts through light woodland of birch, gean and broom. The path is rough but clear. At the edge of the wood the track fords a burn and then passes through a gate, before climbing steeply, through rough grass and moorland, towards the rugged cliffs of Clova Corrie and the Snub.

The climb gradually eases as the path nears the clear waters of Loch Brandy, held in the steep corrie between the cliffs of the Snub and the slopes of Green Hill. Cut right, past the bumpy moorland and peaty lochans to the south of the loch, and then climb up the steep ridge to the east of the loch. The views from the top are excellent: north-west to Lochnagar and the other peaks between Glen Clova, Glen Dee and Glen Shee; south-east to the foot of Glen Clova and the North Sea, and down into the pellucid waters of Loch Brandy.

Cut west around the head of the Corrie, then south down the steep path on the face of the Snub. Rejoin the original path and return to Clova.

One possible extension to this route is to cut south-east, around the Corrie of Loch Wharral, and then to drop back down to the road two miles from Clova.

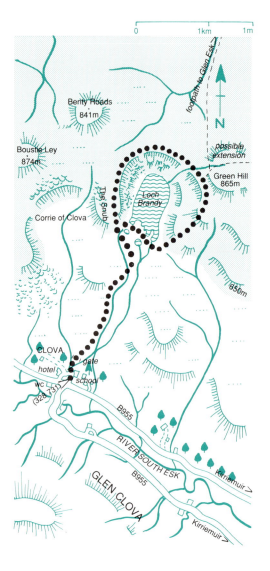

33 Glendoll

Length: Any length
Height climbed: Up to 1800ft (560m)
Grade: A/B/C
Public conveniences: Car park
Public transport: None

Forest walks, plus a number of longer, hill tracks. Paths and views variable. Scenery terrific.

The River North Esk takes its headwaters from the high hills between Glas Maol and Lochnagar. The tributary streams flow through high, shallow glens, before dropping steeply into the great rocky corries carved by the glaciers at the head of Glen Clova; foaming through these rough canyons and then joining at Braedownie to meander listlessly through the alluvium of Glen Clova.

To reach the glen, follow the signs from Kirriemuir; through Dykehead and on up the B955 to Clova. Above Clova a narrow, winding road leads to the car park above the confluence of the streams.

Much of the land in the upper glens has been planted with conifers, and there are a number of forest walks signposted in the area, including short routes of various lengths by the White Water in Glendoll, and two climbs to viewpoints:

one up Red Craig, to the east of Braedownie, and one on the lower slopes of Cairn Broadlands. The latter can be extended along a well-trodden path which leads up to the edge of the forestry, cuts left along the forest edge, then right, up a steep buttress of Cairn Broadlands, to a high pass. This is tough going, but the views are excellent.

Another fine route leads from the Glendoll forest walks, up the Fee Water to the spectacular, cliff-ringed Corrie of Fee, with a dramatic waterfall at its head.

These apart, serious hill-walkers may be tempted by one of the three major hill paths which converge in the glen: the Kilbo path to Glen Prosen, Jock's Road up to Braemar, and Capel Mounth, crossing into Glen Muick *(21)*. **None of these last routes should be attempted without proper maps and equipment.**

34 *Mount Blair*

Length: 4 miles (6.5km) there and back
Height climbed: 1500ft (450m)
Grade: A
Public conveniences: None
Public transport: Bus service from Kirriemuir and Alyth

A stiff hill climb over rough ground. No clear paths. Excellent views from the top.

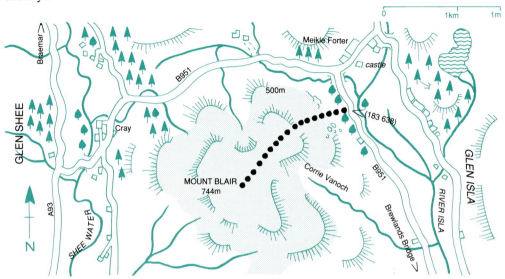

Glen Isla is the most westerly of the Glens of Angus; running southwards some 17 miles from the great cliff-ringed corries of the glens of Caenlochan and Canness (now part of the Caenlochan National Nature Reserve), where the headwaters of the Isla are gathered in the shade of Glas Maol, to the broad valley of Strathmore. The Isla eventually drains to the south-west and joins the Tay near Meikleour.

Thirteen miles west of Kirriemuir on the B951 road (which eventually joins the A93 road through Glenshee and Braemar) is Brewlands Bridge, where the road crosses the River Isla. Two miles north of the bridge, on the same road, there is a large area available for parking to the left of the road. To the left is the flank of Mount Blair; the hill which seperates Glenshee and Glen Isla at their closest point.

There is no clear path up the steep bottom section of the climb. Head westwards, out of the birch woodland and up the hill, between the low cliffs to the right and rocks to the left. Paths start to appear from this point on but they are often simply animal tracks and are unreliable, so it is best to do your own navigation. Climb up to the north-eastern peak of the hill and then walk south-west, by an old fence along a peaty bridge, to the summit. Either return by the same route or by dropping down to the A951, which runs to the north of the hill, and walking back along the road. Just off the road, and visible from the hill, is the ruined castle at Meikle Forter; at one time a stronghold of the Earl of Airlie, but destroyed by the Earl of Argyll in 1640, during the Wars of the Covenant.

Walk 34

35 Cat Law

Length: 4 miles (6.5km) there and back
Height climbed: 1250ft (380m)
Grade: B
Public conveniences: None
Public transport: None

A gentle, moorland hill climb on a rough track. Views excellent.

Cat Law sits on the southern edge of the hills of Angus; just to the Highland side of the Highland Line, looking south and east across the farmland of Strathmore. In fact, there are two parallel Highland Lines at this point; both travelling south-west to north-east and passing to either side of Loch Lintrathen, creating a corrugated belt of ridges and valleys running along the axis.

To reach Cat Law, drive north-west from the centre of Kirriemuir on the B955, signposted for Glen Prosen and Glen Clova. On the outskirts of the town, cut onto the unnumbered road signposted to 'Pearsie'. Turn off this road at the signpost for 'Balintore' and follow a narrow road up the steep, narrow valley of the Quharity Burn to Knowhead Farm (to the left of the road) and, just beyond, the gates to Balintore Castle (to the right). Parking space is a little thin, but try to find some spot which will not interfere with the access of farm vehicles.

To start the walk, cut through a gate into a field, almost directly opposite the farm. Diagonally ahead of the gate, up the slope of the field, is another gate. Pass through this and start climbing up the rough track beyond, as it rises out of the glen of a small tributary of the Quharity Burn and continues over rough moorland towards the rounded, peaty summit. Watch out for lapwing and curlew along this path and, nearer the top, mountain hare and red grouse.

The splendid view includes the towns of Kirriemuir and Forfar in Strathmore, with the line of the Sidlaws beyond; and, towards the Highlands, the hills of Angus and the summit of Lochnagar.

Return by the same route.

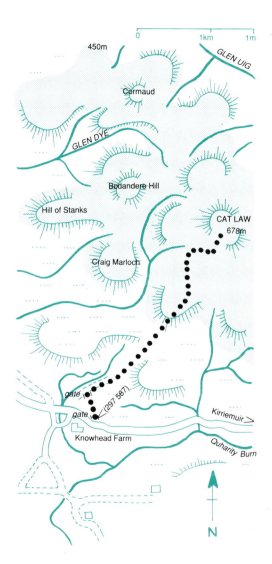

36 Forfar

Length: 1) 3 miles (5km); **2)** up to 3 miles (5km)
Height climbed: 1) None; **2b)** 350ft (100m)
Grade: C (both)
Public conveniences: Forfar
Public transport: Bus services from all directions

1) A short walk on good paths around a small inland loch; 2) A gentle climb up a wooded hill.

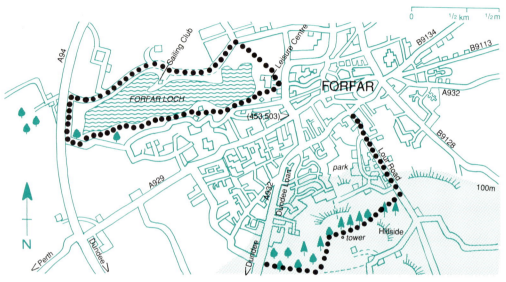

Forfar is a typically douce Scottish town, situated on the edge of the farmland of Strathmore. It is a royal burgh and the old county town of Angus (previously Forfarshire).

1) To the west of the town is Forfar Loch. Follow the main north road from the town centre and turn left at the sign for 'Lochside Leisure Centre'. Walk north from the centre, across parkland, to join the track along the loch side which extends to the west of North Loch Road.

Once on this track the route is simple; along the northern edge of the loch – passing the sailing club – cutting south in the shadow of the A94, and then east, through woodland and parkland, back to the leisure centre. There is a variety of woodland around the loch, and a large number of woodland and water birds.

2) From the lochside, a prominent monument is visible on a hill to the south of the town. This is

a war memorial and there are a number of paths *(see map)* leading up the hill towards it. On the top of the hill, apart from the monument, there is a narrow wood (largely comprised of pine trees), a shelter and a viewpoint, with a view-finder naming the prominent features in the extensive view; including the peaks of Lawers, Schiehallion, and Lochnagar, and, nearer at hand, Glamis Castle, the Airlie Monument (Glen Clova), Forfar and Forfar Loch.

From the eastern end of the hill, three sites of historic interest are visible. To the north-east are Finavon and Turin Hills: both the sites of iron-age forts; while to the east is the semi-forested Dunnichen Hill: the site of the battle of Nechtansmere where, in AD 685, the Picts killed King Egfrid of Northumbria and destroyed his army.

37 Lunan Bay

Length: 6 miles (9.5km) to Ethie Haven and back
Height climbed: Negligible
Grade: A/B/C
Public conveniences: None
Public transport: Bus service between Montrose
and Dundee stops at Hawkhill (1 mile distant)

A walk along a sand beach, with possible extensions along cliff-tops.

To reach this walk from Arbroath drive four miles
north on the A92, and then turn right, at
Inverkeilor, on the unnumbered road signposted to
Lunan. Turn right to the north of the bridge over
the Lunan Water to reach the car park, hidden
amongst the dunes behind the wide, sand beach. In
addition, there is a minor road leading south from
Montrose directly to Lunan.

A path leads through the dunes to the mile
long stretch of beach between the cliffs to the
north and the Lunan Water to the south. The river
is too deep and wide to be forded dry-shod, so, to
reach the southern beach, walk back up to the road
and cut left. After ¼ mile a gate opens into a
stand of trees on a hill. Climb up through these to
reach the ruins of Red Castle. This seems to have
been built in the 15th or 16th century, but now
only a tower and a wall remain; the soft red
sandstone pitted by the erosion of wind and water.

On the far side of the hill a gate opens on to a
lane. Turn left to reach the beach. It is a little
under two miles from the River Lunan to Ethie
Haven.

The first part of the walk is along a broad
beach, with a number of salmon nets stretched
between high wooden posts above the low-water
mark. At the south end of the sands there is a
group of beach huts around the mouth of a small
burn. Cut right through the huts and climb up the
grassy bank beyond on a rough path. After a short
distance this joins a broader track and cuts down
to Ethie Haven: a row of fishermen's houses
behind a tiny natural harbour – one of the few on
the coast.

Beyond Ethie Haven there is a rough track
along the cliff-tops as far as Auchmithie and
Arbroath beyond *(39)*.

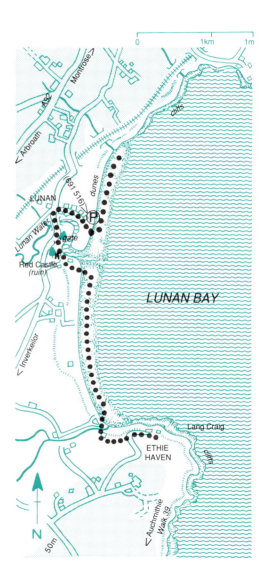

Walk 37

38 Two Arbroath Walks

Length: 1) 5 miles (8km) there and back;
2) 3 miles (5km) there and back
Height climbed: Negligible
Grade: C
Public conveniences: Arbroath
Public transport: Bus and train services

Two short, clear paths through the farmland and woodland around Arbroath.

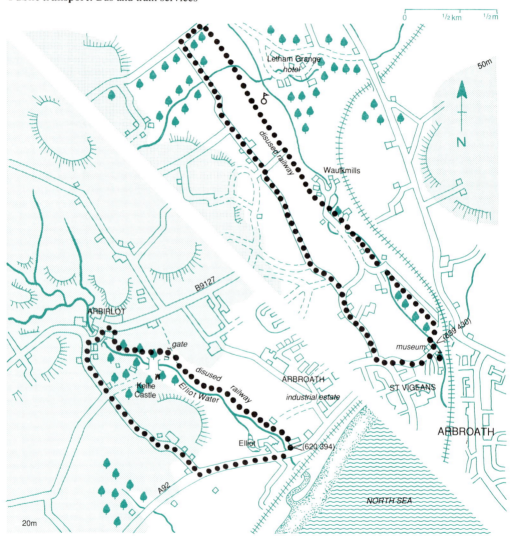

Walk 38

The harbour town of Arbroath, sitting on the Angus coast at the point where it starts to curve in from the North Sea towards the Firth of Tay to the south, is a centre for tourism and industry, but it is best known as a fishing port and is particularly noted for its smoked fish: Abroath smokies and kippers. The harbour area remains busy and vibrant.

The main architectural feature of Abroath is the abbey; founded in 1178 by William the Lion and dedicated to Thomas of Canterbury. As was generally the case with large mediaeval ecclesiastical buildings, the construction of the abbey was spread over hundreds of years, and additions were still being made as late as the 15th century. In time, and hastened by the change of attitudes following the Reformation, the abbey fell into disuse and disrepair. All that now remains is a massive sandstone ruin.

Arbroath's greatest historical moment is connected with the abbey, where, in 1320, the Declaration of Arbroath – the equivalent of a declaration of independence – was signed. The declaration takes the form of a letter written to Pope John XXII.

Another strong link with the past is provided by the tiny museum at St Vigeans, on the northern edge of the town. The museum houses a collection of Pictish carvings: both the 5th- and 6th-century incised symbol stones, and the 7th- to 9th-century Christian relief carvings. Even these later stones include some of the unique, and now indecipherable, Pictish symbols which characterise these peculiar works of art.

Angus was one of the cultural centres of the Pictish kingdom before Kenneth MacAlpin, the King of the Scots, came to power in 843. Following the amalgamation cf the Picts and Scots all signs of Pictish culture, including the carvings, swiftly disappeared.

1) The first of these two walks starts at St Vigeans. The path is quite clear; running straight through a narrow strip of mixed woodland, with farmland beyond on either side. Near the end of the path, the golf course and hotel of Letham Grange are visible to the right.

To return, either retrace the same route, or turn left along a public road, then first left again down a narrow, unnumbered road back to St Vigeans.

2) At the southern end of Arbroath is Elliot, at the foot of the Elliot Water. Another footpath – once again based on a disused railway line – runs up the side of the Elliot Water to the tiny village of Arbirlot.

The path starts through shady woodland, with a bank to the right and a shallow river to the left. After a short distance the track leaves the woodland, goes through a gate, cuts across a field, then passes through a second gate. The path now runs beside the woodland around the deepening gorge of the river. A quarter of a mile after the second gate the path cuts left, off the railway line, through a metal gate. To the left at this point the 15th-century Kelly Castle may be visible, across the water, if the trees are not in leaf.

At the end of the path there is a pretty, single-span bridge over the river at the pleasant village of Arbirlot.

Either return by the same route, or cut left, across the bridge (noting the millstone set into the graveyard wall across the road), then left again at the junction to return to Arbroath by public roads (there is no pavement for most of the way). From the road there are good views across the surrounding farmland to the North Sea.

39 Arbroath Cliffs

Length: 6½ miles (10km)
Height climbed: Negligible
Grade: B
Public conveniences: Arbroath
Public transport: Bus and train services to
Arbroath, and bus link with Auchmithie

A cliff-top walk on paths of varying quality.
Views excellent.

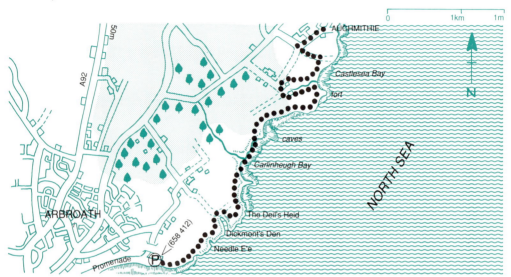

The cliffs of Angus, though not as high as some,
are as dramatic as any. The sandstone from which
they are formed not only gives them their fine red
colour, but is also soft enough to have been
washed into a multitude of inlets, geos, caves and
arches.

The first 1½ miles of the path is along a
Nature Trail, north from Arbroath (a booklet is
available locally). Beyond this there is a further
path of 1½ miles, in less good condition, to the
little port of Auchmithie. Even beyond
Auchmithie a rough track can be followed a
further four miles to Ethie Haven and Lunan Bay
(37).

Start the walk at the north end of the
Arbroath Promenade. There is a car park along the
waterfront. Arbroath is a handsome fishing town,
best known for its ruined abbey, founded in 1178,
where the Declaration of Arbroath – the Scottish

Declaration of Independence – was signed in the
14th century.

The path is clear as far as the caves at the
north end of Carlingheugh Bay. Along the way it
passes such features as the narrow inlet of
Dickmont's Den, the Needle E'e – a sandstone arch
lying parallel to the shore – and the Deil's Heid
stack.

To join the path to Auchmithie, climb up to
the top of the grassy cliff behind the bay and cut to
the right. Much of the rest of the path is through
farmland, and it is important to walk along the
edges of the fields to prevent damage to crops.

The cliffs are rich with plant life and seabirds
are present in huge numbers; including herring
gull, guillemot, shag, cormorant, eider and puffin.
In addition, house martins nest in holes in the
cliffs.

40 Crombie

Length: 2 ½ miles (4km)
Height climbed: Negligible
Grade: C
Public conveniences: Ranger Centre
Public transport: None

A short walk on signposted tracks, through mixed woodland around a small loch. Paths good.

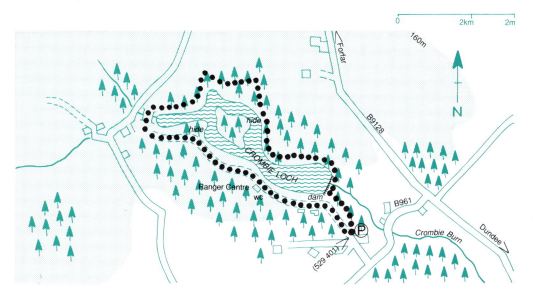

Crombie Country Park sits in the rich farmland behind the south Angus coast between Dundee and Arbroath, with the last ripples of the Sidlaw Hills dying into the fields to the west.

To reach the park drive east on the A92 Arbroath road from Dundee for some 10 miles to Muirdrum, then turn left, onto the B9128 to Forfar, and then left again onto the B961 back towards Dundee. A short distance along this road, on the right hand side, is the entrance to the park. There is a car park set in the trees, a little back from the road, and an honesty box for the small parking fee.

The centerpiece of the park is the manmade Crombie Loch, which attracts a number of species of waterfowl, including great-crested grebe, coot and moorhen. There are two hides set beside the loch.

The route is clearly signposted through the wood. It starts by cutting into the thickly planted trees to the north of the car park along a narrow path, and then leads, along the edge of a narrow, wooded glen, to the dam at the foot of the loch. Cut right across the dam and then continue through the Scots pine along the water's edge beyond.

At the western end of the loch the water becomes shallow. There is a large pine-covered island and marshy ground by the water's edge. This is the most likely place to see a nesting grebe; sitting on its large, untidy nest of floating vegetation.

On the southern edge of the loch there is a Ranger Centre and a small exhibition listing the wide variety of wildlife which can be seen in the woods and on the water.

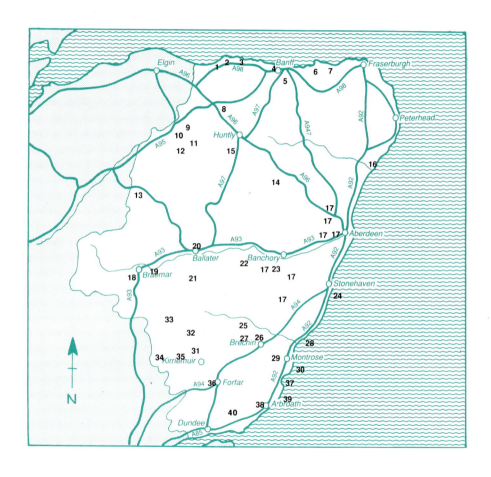

Elgin A96 1 2 3 A98 Banff 4 6 7 Fraserburgh
5 A98
8 A97 A92 Peterhead
9 A96
10 A947
11 Huntly A92 16
12 15
A35 A96
14 A97 A96 17
13 17
17 17 Aberdeen
20 A93 A93 A92
Ballater Banchory
22 17 23 17 Stonehaven
18 19 21 24
Braemar
A93 17
33 A94
32 25 A92
27 26 28
31 Brechin 29 Montrose
34 35 30
Kirriemuir 37
A94 36 Forfar A92 39
38 Arbroath
40
Dundee
A85

N